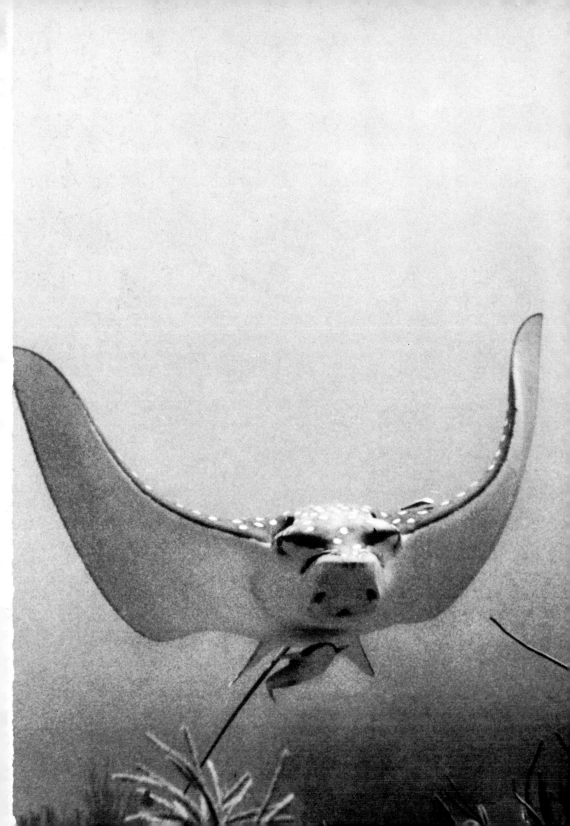

A Chanticleer Press Edition

EARL S. HERALD

FISHES
OF NORTH
AMERICA

Doubleday & Company, Inc., New York

ANIMAL LIFE OF NORTH AMERICA SERIES

Birds of North America
by Austin L. Rand

Fishes of North America
by Earl S. Herald

Insects of North America
by Alexander and Elsie Klots

Invertebrates of North America
by Lorus and Margery Milne

Mammals of North America
by Robert T. Orr

Reptiles and Amphibians of North America
by Alan Leviton

Half-title page photograph: Eagle ray.

Title-page photograph: Barred grunt.

All rights reserved under International and
Pan-American Copyright Conventions.

Published in the United States by Doubleday &
Company, Inc., New York. Distributed in Canada
by Doubleday Canada Limited, Toronto.

Planned and produced by Chanticleer Press, Inc., New York.

Manufactured by Amilcare Pizzi, S.p.A., Milan, Italy.

Library of Congress Catalog Card Number 79–147–353.

Contents

Preface

In recent years there has emerged a new kind of aquatic scientist, the diving biologist. With the development of improved precision underwater photographic equipment, the diving biologist, aided by many skilled and dedicated amateurs, has been able to record and interpret the mysteries of aquatic life in a way never before possible. The diver's study of fishes in their natural habitat is limited by the amount of time he can normally spend on the bottom without lengthy decompression—$2^1/_2$ to 4 hours per day at 50 feet with intermittent dives. A great breakthrough for the biologist has been the development of saturation diving techniques and the use of underwater habitats such as the 1970 Tektite II (at St. John, Virgin Islands; depth 50 feet). This has enabled the diving biologist to live on the bottom for as long as two weeks and to spend as much as eight diving hours a day studying the sequence of innumerable changes in the fauna and flora. For depths greater than those generally reached by the diver, small submarines as well as surface-operated underwater television systems have greatly broadened the horizons for the study of fishes. Thanks to many generous colleagues, information from various underwater study programs has been incorporated in this volume.

Under the watchful guidance of editor Milton Rugoff and associate editor Joanne Shapiro, Chanticleer Press has assembled a remarkable series of photographs which make this volume on the North American fish fauna vastly more interesting. Mrs. Lillian Dempster has provided technical assistance, and final typing has been ably accomplished by Miss Judy McClenahan. Like many ichthyologists, I understand fish much better than I do English, so it has been the painstaking task of my wife, Olivia, to make the text readable. To these as well as the many other friends and diving associates who have provided assistance—my humble thanks.

EARL S. HERALD
Steinhart Aquarium
San Francisco

Bay pipefish (Syngnathus griseolineatus); Pacific marine.

Introduction

The success of the fishes in adapting themselves to various habitats is well shown by their distribution in all the waters of the world: they are found everywhere except in waters that are toxic. It is difficult to be sure how many species of fishes there actually are, but recent estimates place the number at around 21,500. These are divided into approximately 36 orders and more than 400 families. The difference between salt and fresh water has proved a physiological barrier to most kinds of fishes, yet others have managed to adapt, and move back and forth between the two kinds of water without difficulty. The most rigid living requirements among fishes are undoubtedly those concerned with spawning. Fresh-water fishes living in the ocean, such as the salmon, always return to fresh water to spawn, and saltwater fishes living in fresh water, such as some of the gobies of the Pacific islands, always return to the ocean to spawn. Only a very few, like certain species of the African mouthbrooder genus *Tilapia*, are able to spawn in salt, brackish, or fresh water.

We think of a typical fish as having scales, and yet there are many that lack them. We know that fishes are found in water, but there are a number that spend a great deal of time out of water. Most fishes have gills and respire by absorbing oxygen from the water as it passes over the gill filaments, but there are exceptions that have only vestigial gills that are often inadequate for respiration; in these fishes, breathing may be carried out by a lung, or by vascular areas above the gills and in the mouth that absorb oxygen directly from the air. Fishes usually have fins on the top of the back, on the tail, and under the body behind the vent, as well as paired pectoral (arm) fins and paired pelvic (leg) fins, but certain fishes, lack some or all of these. So we must look at the internal anatomy to find out why a fish is classified as a fish. Fishes are vertebrates; all have a supporting structure down the back. In the primitive forms it is a cartilaginous rod; in the more complex fishes it becomes partially or wholly ossified to form a backbone. The heart of most fishes has two chambers, as contrasted with three or four chambers for the higher vertebrates.

Sensory organs among the fishes show a tremendous amount of variation. For example, fish vision varies from amazingly acute perception to complete blindness. Sensitive barbels and other tactile organs on the head and body sometimes compensate for lack of sight in the blind species. In the muddy waters of Africa and South America there are fishes, such as mormyrids and knifefishes, which have small electric organs that discharge impulses that tell the fish about its surroundings.

In certain fishes, especially the sharks, the sense of smell is very important in locating food. Experiments with blocking the nostrils of salmons returning to fresh water to spawn revealed that a salmon's ability to find its parent stream is dependent upon its sense of smell.

The sense of taste is important to some fishes in locating food. Certain catfishes of the genus *Ictalurus* have taste buds covering most of the outside of the body; food coming in contact with these taste buds is quickly devoured. Along the sides of the body many fishes have a lateral line or a system of lines, usually in the form of a tube with a series of pores that open to the outside. These pores lead to sensory cells that register vibrations in the water, thus effectively alerting the fish to predators or prey. The equilibrium system of fishes is found in the semicircular canals of the inner ear, hidden in the brain case.

The air bladder is usually essential to the fishes in which it is present. It is located in the upper part of the abdominal cavity and is used as a hydrostatic organ, enabling the fish to float at any given level without sinking or rising. It may also function as a resonance chamber in sound production, and in some fishes it has a respiratory function.

Most reproduction in the fish world is by means of external fertilization, in which the eggs spewed out by the female are fertilized at the same time by spermatozoa, known as milt, extruded in the immediate area by the male. There are, however, a number of live-bearers and some egg-layers that practice internal fertilization. Some fishes, too, are ovoviviparous, that is, eggs with definite shells hatch within the body of the female and the young are born alive.

Temperature is often a factor both in north-south or latitudinal distribution and in vertical, or depth, distribution. Although the temperature-tolerance range of an individual species may be less than 15° F., the total range of all species is from freezing waters to those of more than 100°. The temperature of the fish's body fluctuates with the temperature of the surrounding water. This fluctuation of body temperature with environment is also found among the amphibians and reptiles; in contrast, the body temperature of the higher vertebrates, the birds and the mammals, is fairly uniform.

Air temperatures of winter and summer change the water temperature and, in so doing, may change the vertical distribution of various species; some fishes have sharply defined temperature preferences. For example, intertidal and shallow-water fishes in the Puget Sound area of Washington may be found in

Overleaf: Upstream migrant sockeye salmon (Oncorhynchus nerka) returning to parent stream to spawn and die; British Columbia.

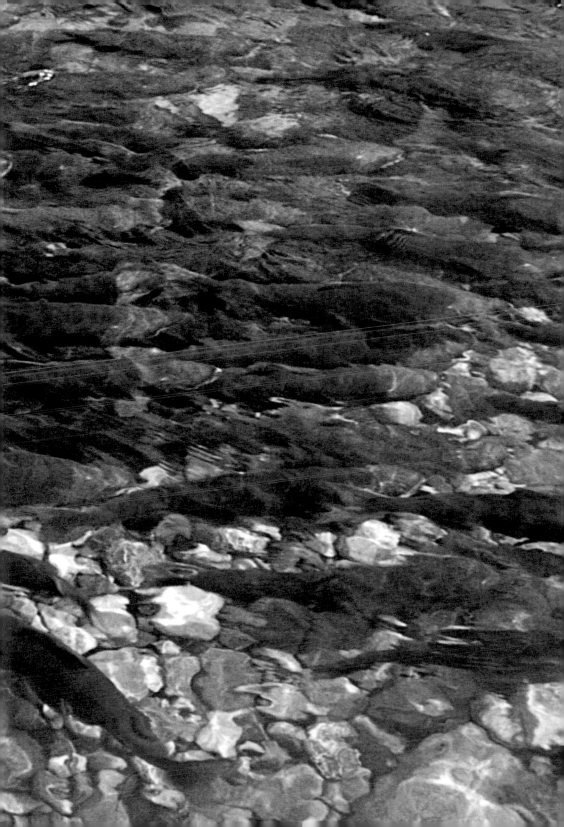

a similar temperature layer or isotherm in the San Francisco and Monterey area, but that temperature will probably be at a depth of about 600 feet.

In small bodies of water, current usually has limited effect in determining distribution of fresh-water fishes, but for marine fishes on both the Atlantic and Pacific coasts, current is a major distributional factor.

On the Atlantic coast the warm Gulf Stream traveling northward may provide subtropical temperatures along much of the coastline as far north as Cape Hatteras. Farther north are temperate and then colder waters. These are also, of course, affected by summer and winter air temperatures. On the Pacific coast, the eastward-flowing cold North Pacific current divides at Point Conception, moving northward toward Oregon and southward toward Baja California. These current patterns mean that for a given latitude there will be more warm-water fishes on the Atlantic coast than on the Pacific. In looking at the map, we find that San Diego, California, is about on the same latitude as Charleston, South Carolina; but because of the current, the elements of the subtropical fauna will be very limited on the Pacific coast as compared with those of the Atlantic. For example, in the chaetodont family of the beautiful tropical butterflyfishes, there are twelve species listed for the Atlantic shores of the United States and only two for the Pacific.

The Gulf of California, often called the Sea of Cortez, presents some special problems. Because of currents, the water temperatures on the outside of the peninsula of Baja California are often colder than they are in southern California. Thus, one must travel almost to Cape San Lucas of the Baja peninsula before the tropical Pacific fauna is encountered. In the Cape region there are about 600 species of fishes, while there are only about half that number in the north end of the Gulf.

Fish classification is always subject to changes, with professional ichthyologists constantly providing many new ideas. The systematic arrangement used in this book is largely that of Greenwood, Rosen, Weitzman, and Myers, which appeared in 1966.[1] This has subsequently been followed by many authors and to a major extent by the 1970 "List of Common and Scientific Names of Fishes from the United States and Canada" (Special Publication No. 6 of the American Fisheries Society). The latter is a most useful volume, showing the principal members of the American ichthyofauna north of Mexico.

To understand fishes it will be helpful to review a few basic elements of fish anatomy and terminology. For that reason, anatomical diagrams and a glossary are included at the end of this text.

1. Phyletic studies of teleostean fishes with a provisional classification of living forms. *Bulletin of the American Museum of Natural History*, Volume 131, Part 4, pages 341–455.

Jawless Fishes *(Class Agnatha)*

Two kinds of living fishes, the hags and the lampreys, make up this very primitive and well-adapted group. They are often called the cyclostomes, a term derived from the circular appearance of the suctorial mouth with its pointed teeth. Although the number of species is small, perhaps no more than 45, they have been able to survive with a lack of certain anatomical characteristics that would probably prove fatal in more advanced forms; they lack bones, jaws, paired limbs and girdles, a sympathetic nervous system, a spleen, and scales. Support of the body is provided by cartilage or fibrous material, with an unsegmented notochord serving the same purpose as the backbone in higher fishes. Respiration takes place in a series of six to fourteen gill pouches, which may open individually or through a common tube to the throat and the outside. There is only a single nostril. Fertilization is external. Some species of lampreys are restricted to a marine habitat, while others occur only in fresh water or in both fresh and salt water. Hagfishes are found only in the ocean.

Because of their many exceptional characteristics, the hags and lampreys are generally placed in separate orders, the Myxiniformes and the Petromyzontiformes.

Hagfishes (Family Myxinidae)

The hagfish is a voracious scavenger—a blind, elongate, wormlike fish usually less than 30 inches long, with a slightly rounded tail and several thick, fingerlike whiskers extending from around the mouth. Two rows of sharp, broadly triangular teeth, the number of which is useful in species identification, lead to a simple, tubelike digestive tract.

For many years hags were thought to be hermaphroditic, but research has shown that although both sex organs may be present in any given individual, only one organ, either testis or ovary, is functional; the other remains in a rudimentary state. An amazing physiological characteristic of the hag can sometimes be seen if it is handled roughly and then dropped into a bucket of water. In a short time the water will be entirely converted to a slimy mucus, a result of the activity of many mucous pores along the sides of the body. The hag has for this reason often been called the slime eel. About twenty species of hags are recognized. They are found in temperate or cold sea water no warmer than 55° F. Usually they do not survive in brackish or fresh water. Their depth range is from 100 to 3,100 feet.

Occasionally when a haddock fisherman begins to examine his catch on deck, he discovers that some of the fishes are hollow—veritable "bags of bones." When he shakes one of these vigorously, out tumbles the culprit: a hagfish. This unwelcome intruder, having drilled into the fish with its rasplike teeth, has worked like a termite, leaving the exterior intact but consuming most of the edible interior portions.

In some areas hags are extremely abundant. They are usually found in soft mud or clay bottoms, where they spend a good part of the time embedded with only the snout and some of the whiskers protruding. In the aquarium, the hag usually remains coiled on the bottom of the tank; sometimes it will even tie itself into a knot. Food is located entirely by smell. When progressing toward a food scent, the hag emerges from the mud and swims horizontally with an undulating motion. Biologists have learned that it will swim toward a trap constructed from a five-gallon can baited with a few putrid fish heads. Many holes driven into the can with a large spike permit the odor of the bait to be disseminated in all directions; these openings also let the slender-bodied hag squeeze into the can, but do not let it escape.

Lampreys (Family Petromyzontidae)

The eel-like sea lamprey *(Petromyzon marinus)* is normally a marine species that occurs on both sides of the Atlantic and migrates into fresh water to spawn. Gradually it has moved into the Great Lakes and become firmly established there; but because of the serious economic loss resulting from the depredations of these fishes, which are parasitic, a widespread research and control program has been initiated in the Great Lakes region. Although it is capable of rapid, undulating swimming, the sea lamprey does much of its traveling attached to a host fish while sucking out its life juices. It attaches itself to the victim with its piercing teeth and keeps the victim's blood in a fluid state by means of an anticoagulating substance in its saliva. Sea lampreys ingest only blood, whereas some of the fresh-water species also ingest a small amount of flesh.

During March, April, and May, *Petromyzon marinus* usually moves into shallow-water streams to spawn. Having located a rocky bottom suitable for spawning, a male and female usually prepare the nest together. As the female lays as many as 200,000 eggs, the male, wound around her, spews spermatozoa,

Sea lamprey (Petromyzon marinus); Atlantic marine and fresh-water.

known as milt, over the nest. Shortly thereafter the parents die. In about two weeks the eggs hatch into blind, toothless, wormlike larvae known as ammocoetes. Four to six years later these ammocoetes begin their transformation into true lampreys. During this radical metamorphosis many anatomical changes take place. The rudimentary eyes become functional, and soon the changing ammocoete acquires a new kind of mouth with a full complement

Sand tiger shark (Odontaspis taurus) with two remoras attached; Atlantic marine.

of 112 to 125 horny, rasplike teeth. The digestive tract is altered, and the bile duct and gall bladder disappear. Following these changes, the youngster starts its move downstream and into the parasitic phase of its life history. The adult *Petromyzon marinus* reaches a maximum length of about 3 feet.

The lamprey family contains about 25 species. Some, such as the western American *Lampetra ayresi*, are confined entirely to fresh water, but all of them have a life history similar to that of *P. marinus*. In the United States and Canada there are actually fourteen species of lampreys, six of which are parasitic and eight nonparasitic. The major difference in the two forms is that the non-parasitic lampreys do not feed as adults; as a result they never grow larger than the larvae from which they are transformed.

An adult lamprey looks so much like an eel that one of the names often

applied is "lamprey eel." It is not related to the true eels, however; it lacks the jaws and many other characteristics of the more advanced fishes. The adult lamprey has seven pairs of gill pouches supported by a complex cartilaginous structure known as the branchial basket. The digestive tract has on one side a small ridge which is probably the forerunner of the spiral valve, or typhlosole, of the sharks and rays. The ear has only two semicircular canals. Depending upon the genus, there may be one or two dorsal fins, and these are separate from the tail fin. Identification of species is often based on teeth arrangement.

The use of lampreys as food has had an erratic history. In the Middle Ages they were considered a delicacy. Although lampreys are no longer fished for food, they were sold in markets in New England as late as the 1850's. The larvae can be used as bait.

Cartilaginous Fishes *(Class Chondrichthyes)*

In this zoological class, which includes sharks, skates, rays, and chimaeroids, the cartilage skeleton is present but further developed than in the hags and lampreys. These chondrichthian fishes have a well-developed lower jaw, and both jaws have bony teeth. Sharks, skates, and rays have an upper jaw that is separate from the cranium although it may be attached at certain points, while the upper jaw of the chimaeroids is permanently fused to the cranium. The circulatory system has a series of heart valves preceded by a chamber, the *bulbus conus arteriosus*. The spleen is present, but the air bladder is absent. The fins are paired. The scales, of the type known as placoid, are developed in the same manner as a tooth, and in this respect are entirely different from the scales of bony fishes. The gills have five, six, or seven individual openings, or clefts, to the outside. Female chondrichthians are fertilized internally, and for this purpose the males are equipped with paired claspers attached just forward of the vent. Almost 600 species of sharks, skates, rays, and chimaeroids belong to this class.

SHARKS *(Superorder Selachii)*

Sharks have five to seven gill clefts on each side of the head, usually in front of and slightly above the pectoral fins; in the rays, the five clefts are on the underside of the pectorals, which are greatly enlarged and expanded. Sharks breathe like the bony fishes, taking water in through the mouth and passing it out over the gills; the rays bring water in through the spiracles on the top of the head and expel it through the gills. The free eyelid on the upper portion of the eye of a shark is lacking in the skates and rays, and there are a number of internal anatomical features that are equally distinctive. All sharks have lopsided, or heterocercal, tails, in which the upper lobe is much longer than the lower. About 250 kinds of sharks are known.

Frill Shark *(Family Chlamydoselachidae)*

In appearance, the very slender frill shark *(Chlamydoselachus anguineus)* is very suggestive of a marine snake or monster. The very large mouth filled with many sharp and fearsome teeth adds to this impression. The dorsal and anal fins are small and located just in front of the tail. The tail itself bears no resemblance to the typical, lopsided shark tail; the ventral lobe is invisible, and the elongate upper lobe extends backward like a broadened whip.

One of the features that most clearly differentiates the frill shark from the sixgill cowshark is the nature of the six gill slits. On the frill shark, the first gill opening extends under the neck from one side to the other; on the sixgill cowshark, the six gill slits are normal and do not extend under the throat.

A number of frill sharks have been caught off Japan, and two have been taken off California, one of which was captured in a surface gill net. The remainder have been taken from the European coasts between Norway and Portugal. Capture depths were usually greater than 1,500 feet, and the stomach contents revealed deep-water octopuses and squids.

Cowsharks (Family Hexanchidae)

By counting the number of gill openings along the side of a shark's head we can determine very quickly whether we are dealing with a primitive shark belonging to the sixgill and sevengill cowshark family or with one of the remaining families of sharks, nearly all of which have five gill openings. The adult sixgill cowshark (Hexanchus griseus) has a broad head, a heavy, thick body, and a very long tail. Its color ranges from shades of nondescript gray to brown, with no distinctive markings. These giant, deep-water sharks sometimes weigh as much as 1,700 pounds, and reach an estimated length of 17 feet.

The sixgill has a wide distribution; on the Pacific coast of North America it is known from British Columbia to southern California, and it is also found along the Chilean coast of South America. It has not been taken in the central Pacific, although it is known from Japan to Australia, from the Indian Ocean, and from South Africa. It is also found on both coasts of the Atlantic and in the Mediterranean. Despite the fact that it has been caught in depths greater than one mile, it also occurs in shallow water. Strangely, on the American Pacific coast it rarely enters San Francisco Bay (only two specimens have been caught there), yet it commonly occurs in Tomales Bay, only a few miles to the north and much shallower. The young, which are born alive, are surprisingly small when compared with the adults: some measure no more than 16 inches.

The Pacific sevengill (Notorynchus maculatus) swims constantly and rarely rests on the bottom. It has a large head, a slender body, and a very long tail. Its teeth are recessed, so that their sharp points and destructive potential are not fully evident until the fish is pulled up on deck. Then one should stand back and beware, for the snapping mouth and thrashing body of even a sevengill measuring no more than 6 feet are very dangerous.

The normal habitat of the Pacific sevengill is offshore waters, and it is seldom caught in shallow water except for the southern end of San Francisco Bay, where a nursery ground is located. The females, with a maximum size of 9 feet and a maximum weight of 300 pounds, come into the bay to drop their young. On the Pacific coast the sevengill ranges from British Columbia to southern California. It has also been recorded from the Mediterranean, the coasts of South Africa, Argentina, Chile, Japan, China, Australia, New Zealand, and the Indian Ocean. But these records may include more than one species.

Sand Tigers (Family Odontaspididae)

Numerous sharp, wicked-looking teeth protruding from the mouth of the sand tiger shark *(Odontaspis taurus)* make this species fit almost perfectly the popular conception of a dangerous shark. Despite its grim appearance, there are no records on the American side of the Atlantic of its having attacked humans. In South Africa, however, it is considered very dangerous and capable of unprovoked attack. Although the sand tiger is primarily a shallow-water shark, it exhibits some characteristics of the deep-water species, swimming almost constantly and seldom resting on the bottom. Although sharks do not have air bladders, the sand tiger has developed the peculiar ability to swallow air and retain it in the stomach, thus allowing the stomach to act as an air bladder or hydrostatic organ. The sand tiger is fairly common on both sides of the Atlantic, but its populations seem to fluctuate with water temperature. Along the American coast its normal range is from the Gulf of Maine to Florida, with an isolated population in Brazil. The largest sand tiger ever caught measured 10 feet 5 inches and is estimated to have weighed more than 300 pounds.

The sand tiger has few relatives—there are only six or seven other species in the family, including the eastern Pacific *O. ferox*, which has been captured in southern California. The others range through the eastern Atlantic and Mediterranean, and on the coasts of Argentina, Australia, Japan, China, and India.

Mackerel Sharks (Family Lamnidae)

"Monsters of the sea" might be a more appropriate name for the mackerel sharks, since this family includes some of the world's most dangerous fishes.

The most widely known is the great white shark *(Carcharodon carcharias)*, commonly called the maneater. Sharks of this group are heavy-bodied and usually have a nearly symmetrical tail, resembling that of the tuna more than the lopsided tail of the typical shark. It is probable that all of these fast-moving sharks swim constantly and do not rest on the bottom at any time. Speed in the water requires careful stabilization, and for this purpose the mackerel sharks have large keels along the sides of the tail just in front of the fin. Further hydrodynamic control is gained by means of the characteristically large pectoral fins, whose length is about equal to that of the head.

Preliminary identification among the mackerel sharks can be made by the profile of the teeth. For example, the upper center teeth of the great white shark, or maneater, are broadly triangular with saw-toothed edges, whereas those of the other mackerel sharks, such as the Atlantic porbeagle *(Lamna nasus)* and the mako *(Isurus oxyrinchus)*, are very slender and quite smooth. One mark that can sometimes be used to distinguish the maneater is a conspicuous black spot in the axil, or base of the pectoral fin. The largest maneater ever caught measured 36 feet 6 inches in length, and was taken at Port Fairey, Australia. There is a record of a 21-foot Cuban specimen weighing 7,100 pounds, with a liver that weighed slightly more than 1,000 pounds.

The maneater is a fish of the open seas and is found less frequently inshore. Despite the fact that it is usually captured near the surface, there is a Cuban record of one from a depth of 4,200 feet. When the maneater is found in very shallow water, it is usually in areas adjacent to deep water. Although it is most abundant in tropical areas around the world, it does range into temperate waters; on the American coasts it has been taken as far north as the State of Washington in the Pacific, and the St. Pierre Bank just south of Newfoundland in the Atlantic. The temperament of the maneater is reputed to be invariably bad. Although it is reported to attack readily anything and everything, skin divers who have encountered this monster have usually survived to tell the tale. There seem to be indications that the maneater may sometimes be just as wary and frightened of the skin diver as the latter is of the maneater.

There are two species of makos: the longfin mako *(Isurus paucus)*, and the more common shortfin mako *(I. oxyrinchus)*. Maximum length for the latter is thought to be about 12 feet, which would probably correspond to a weight of about 1,200 pounds. The largest authenticated record, however, is of an Atlantic mako 10 feet 6 inches long, weighing 1,005 pounds. These sharks have a worldwide distribution in tropical and, to a lesser extent, temperate seas.

Whenever possible, the mako takes its food at one gulp. This is well illustrated by a 120-pound swordfish found intact in the stomach of a 730-pound Bahaman mako. With much larger swordfish, attack is usually made from the rear; the mako can remove the entire tail of the prey with one bite. With its tremendous speed, it is unquestionably a dangerous shark. It has been known to attack small boats, and will attack a swimmer, although it does not have the reputation of being a maneater.

The common Atlantic mackerel shark, or porbeagle *(Lamna nasus)*, has a related species on the American Pacific coast—the salmon shark *(L. ditropis)*. In addition to the differences in the teeth mentioned above, these two species can be distinguished from other members of the mackerel family by the presence of two stabilizing keels, instead of one, along the sides of the tail. The main keel is in the same lateral position as on the mako and the maneater. There is also a small keel just below this, but it is limited to the tail fin. The porbeagle and the salmon shark are thick-bodied like the maneater, but although potentially dangerous, they have not been implicated in attacks on man.

The maneater and the mako are found throughout both temperate and tropical waters, while the Atlantic porbeagle and the Pacific salmon shark are primarily temperate-water species. The salmon shark ranges from Japan and Alaska to southern California. The porbeagle shark is found from the Gulf of St. Lawrence to South Carolina, and on the European coasts from the North Sea to the Mediterranean. It also occurs along the northwestern coasts of Africa. Mackerel sharks with a double tail keel also occur off South America and Australia; although they have been described as a distinct species, further study may show them to be identical with the Pacific *L. ditropis*. Ten feet is usually accepted as the maximum length of the common Atlantic and Pacific mackerel sharks, with the females attaining sexual maturity at about 5 feet.

Thresher Sharks (Family Alopiidae)

An extremely long, whiplike tail approximately equal to the length of the body provides the thresher shark with tremendous driving power, enabling it to round up schools of small fishes by rapidly encircling them. Slapping the surface of the water with its tail also helps it to frighten the fishes into tighter formation so that it can feed on them more easily. In the central Pacific, threshers are often accidentally hooked on deep-set tuna lines, probably when they attempt to herd the dead bait with their tails. Despite its ferocious nature toward schooling fishes, the thresher is entirely harmless to man.

Although the threshers as a group are primarily offshore and tropical in distribution, they do enter temperate waters in considerable numbers. At times during the summer months they are very common off the New England coast; in the Santa Barbara Island area of California they have been fished commercially during the summer.

The thresher family is small, having only a single genus and perhaps four species. The best-known species is the common thresher *(Alopias vulpinus)*, which has an extended distribution on both sides of the Atlantic as well as in the eastern Pacific. In the western Pacific its counterpart is *A. pelagicus*. Other species, such as the bigeye thresher, named for its extremely large eyes, are suspected of being deep-water species; these are undoubtedly often mistaken for the common thresher. Two species of the bigeye have been described, *A. superciliosus*, known from Cuba, Florida, California, and Madeira, and *A. profundus*, from Formosa.

The largest threshers measure more than 20 feet in length and weigh more than 1,000 pounds. The females probably mature at about 14 feet and usually carry only two or four young. The newborn are 4 feet 6 inches to 5 feet long.

Basking Shark (Family Cetorhinidae)

The giant basking shark *(Cetorhinus maximus)*, second only to the whale shark in size, sometimes reaches a length of 45 feet. It can best be described as a mackerel shark that has substituted a plankton diet for a carnivorous one. Like the mackerel sharks, it has a nearly symmetrical, tuna-like tail with heavy lateral supports, or stabilizing keels. Its plankton diet requires it to strain tremendous volumes of water; to do so the basking shark has greatly enlarged gill openings extending from the top of the head and neck almost to the center section of its underside. As the water flows into the mouth and out over the gills, the straining of the plankton is done by many long, slender rakers attached to the inside of each gill arch and extending into the throat. In some basking sharks the gill rakers are dropped during the winter months and then regenerated during the summer.

The record length for the basking shark is usually given as 50 feet, but is probably closer to 45 feet. The average is from 30 to 35 feet. It is believed that the young are born alive and are approximately 5 or 6 feet long. Males mature at a length of 15 or 20 feet. The basking shark has been described from many regions of the world, but most records are from temperate waters. They may occur singly or in schools numbering as many as 100 sharks. Sizable populations exist off the European coasts and off the southern California coast.

The liver in a shark usually makes up at least 10 per cent of its total weight. For example, a 30-foot basker weighing 8,600 pounds would have a liver weighing at least 860 pounds, from which a high yield in oil would be obtained. The greatest volume of oil ever obtained from a single basking shark liver was 600 gallons. The liver oil contains no vitamins and is used chiefly in leather-tanning.

It is somewhat surprising that the two largest fishes are both sharks and that both feed on such a remarkably small-sized food as plankton. In distribution they are somewhat segregated, since the whale shark usually prefers tropical waters while the basking shark is found in more temperate seas. The two are easy to distinguish by the conspicuous white spots present on the back of the whale shark but lacking on the basking shark.

Whale Shark (Family Rhincodontidae)

The whale shark *(Rhincodon typus)*, the largest species of shark, is the only spotted shark that has the mouth at the tip of the head; it has ridges along the sides of the body, and it grows to a length of at least 45 feet. Skin divers report these fishes to be so docile that one can swim around them with impunity. Many articles have been written describing collisions of sailing ships and power vessels with this lethargic shark; in some cases the shark has remained impaled on the bow of the ship for many hours.

Like the massive basking shark, the whale shark feeds on very small food items, ranging from plankton, schools of little fishes and squids, to crustaceans. Whale sharks lay eggs; sixteen eggs were found in a Ceylon specimen, and a living, 14-inch shark in an egg case measuring 12 by 3.5 by 3.5 inches was found in the Gulf of Mexico. Whale sharks are recorded from all tropical waters of the world. On the American Atlantic coasts the center of abundance is the Caribbean region, while occasional individuals have been found as far north as New York and as far south as Brazil. Another population is in the Gulf of California, particularly around Cape San Lucas.

Nurse and Carpet Sharks (Family Orectolobidae)

The sharks in this family are similar in appearance to the scyliorhinid catsharks

Top: Horn shark (Heterodontus francisci); Pacific marine.
Bottom: Nurse shark (Ginglymostoma cirratum); Atlantic-Pacific marine.

but can readily be distinguished from them and all other sharks by a conspicuous pair of grooves, one on each side of the head, running from the mouth to the nostril. Each of the oronasal grooves, as they are called, has a thick, fleshy barbel at its anterior end, which further aids in identification. The carpet shark also has a fringe of fleshy palps around the sides of the head.

The orectolobids have two dorsal fins and spiracles, but lack the nictitating eye membrane common to many other sharks. The tail is not turned upward but is in line with the rest of the body. Most of them are small, inshore forms, but there are a few of the perhaps two dozen species in the family that reach a large size, such as the nurse shark *(Ginglymostoma cirratum)*, which has a maximum length of 14 feet. When full grown, the nurse is quite heavy as well as large; an 8-foot specimen may weigh 350 pounds. This species is common in shallow water from the Florida keys southward to the West Indies and Brazil. It occasionally comes as far north as Cape Lookout, North Carolina, and also occurs along the tropical west African coast. On the Pacific coast it ranges from the Gulf of California to Peru. All other members of the family are found in the tropical areas of the Indian and Pacific oceans.

Under normal circumstances the nurse shark is not considered dangerous; if molested, however, it can become so. There is a record of a Miami skin diver who caught a 5-foot nurse shark by the tail and then let it go, only to have the shark turn and sink its teeth into his thigh. The diver's companions were able, however, to free his leg from the shark's jaws.

The fact that nurse sharks are born alive brings up a curious point about the orectolobid family: in three of the seven genera the young are born alive though in the other four the females lay eggs. The sharks that are born alive are hatched from eggs within the uterus of the mother, which is a type of reproduction called ovoviviparity.

Catsharks *(Family Scyliorhinidae)*

Some of the most beautiful sharks in the world are found among the scyliorhinids, for a number of the species in this large family have picturesque patterns with exotic stripes, bars, and mottling. Most of the catsharks are small, inshore fishes less than 3 feet in length; there are some small deep-water species, however, such as the thirteen members of the genus *Apristurus*, a group found on both sides of the Atlantic as well as in the Pacific.

The scyliorhinids usually have two dorsal fins, and the tail is in a straight line with the rest of the body, not bent upward. Spiracles are present, but there is no nictitating membrane on the eyes, as there is in some other species. In some respects the catsharks are similar to the orectolobid nurse sharks, but they may be distinguished by the fact that as a rule the cats lack the groove between the nostril and the mouth; if this groove is present, as it is in a few species, the fleshy whisker of the nurse shark is lacking. All catsharks lay rectangular eggs that usually have a single tendril attached to each corner.

The Atlantic false catshark *(Pseudotriakis microdon)* is a deep-water species normally occurring at 1,000 to 5,000 feet; however, one of this species did wash ashore on Long Island. The chain dogfish *(Scyliorhinus retifer)* occurs off New Jersey in depths ranging between 240 and 750 feet. Deep-water sharks on the Pacific coast include the 2-foot brown catshark *(Apristurus brunneus)* and the filetail catshark *(Parmaturus xaniurus)*. Although there are other less common middle-water and deep-water species on both Atlantic coasts and on the American Pacific coast, the greatest number of catshark species occur in the Indo-Pacific.

The swell shark is a type of shark that seems quite ordinary in the sea but when pulled out of water blows up like a balloon. Swell sharks are small and inhabit shallow water in both temperate and tropical zones. The maximum length for all six species in the single genus, *Cephaloscyllium,* is around 4 feet. They range throughout the Pacific from California to Chile, Australia, New Zealand, Japan, and Africa, but are absent from the Atlantic. Probably the best-known swell shark is the single California species, *C. ventriosum.* It ranges from Monterey Bay southward into Baja California waters, and to Mazatlán and Chile. In some areas it is common in kelp beds and is often caught in lobster traps. Despite its small size it has a very large mouth with a menacing set of teeth, which are very effective in catching fishes.

Smooth Dogfishes (Family Triakidae)

The smooth dogfishes form a small group intermediate between the nurse sharks and catsharks (families Orectolobidae and Scyliorhinidae) and the requiem sharks (family Carcharinidae); the smooth dogs have the body profile and many of the anatomical characteristics of the latter, but their dentition is more like that of the former. The family includes fewer than thirty species in perhaps seven or eight genera. These sharks are small, usually measuring less than 5 feet; they are inshore species and are often fairly abundant. One of the best known and, in fact, the second most common shark on the American Atlantic coast is the smooth dogfish *(Mustelus canis)*. It ranges all the way from Cape Cod in the north to Brazil and Uruguay in the south. Between Cape Cod and North Carolina there is a seasonal north-south migration pattern which is correlated with water temperature.

The most abundant shark on the American Pacific coast is the drab brown smoothhound *(Mustelus henlei)*. My colleagues and I have data on 7,211 sharks and bat rays caught in San Francisco Bay between 1948 and 1954; of these, 3,076, or 42.5 per cent, were brown smoothhounds. The average length of the males in this group was about 20 inches, and that of the females 31 inches.

Another smooth dogfish, the American Pacific leopard shark *(Triakis semifasciata)*, is brilliantly marked with black saddles across the back. It normally ranges from Oregon to Baja California, and because of its attractive appearance, it has been shipped to public aquariums in many parts of the world.

Requiem Sharks (Family Carcharhinidae)

All members of the requiem shark family have the appearance of "typical sharks." There are two dorsal fins, paired pectoral and pelvic fins, an anal fin, and a long, lopsided tail with the upper lobe much elongated. There are no barbels around the mouth. Spiracles are present in some genera but not in others. The young are born alive. For the most part the members of this family are tropical in distribution. This is the largest family of sharks, with a total of some sixty species distributed among fifteen genera.

The tiger shark *(Galeocerdo cuvieri)* is notorious for its omnivorous food habits. It eats anything available, including mammals, birds, fishes, lobsters, horseshoe crabs, garbage, coal, tin cans, and, finally, people. If sea turtles are available, it consumes them with great relish. The tiger shark can be easily identified by its distinctive markings. The background color is a grayish brown that is lighter on the undersurfaces, and the principal markings are vertical bars along the sides. In addition, there may be a spottiness or mottling, or perhaps a reticulated pattern, along the upper surface of the body. The sides of the pointed teeth are serrated with a deep notch on one side; the base of each one is quite broad. The young may be born at any time of the year.

Sharks have been fished commercially for their livers in many parts of the world, including Florida and the Caribbean. The two most valuable liver sharks were found on the American Pacific coast: the soupfin *(Galeorhinus zyopterus)*

Blue shark (Prionace glauca); Atlantic-Pacific marine.

and the dogfish *(Squalus acanthias)*. The latter also occurs in the Atlantic. Both of these had previously been considered pest sharks because of their depredations on fishermen's nets and catch.

One useful side aspect of the shark fisheries has been that they have made investigations of shark biology possible. More has been learned about the biology of sharks with valuable livers than had been known about any other sharks, skates, rays or chimaeroids. The first surprising discovery was that in the northern part of the soupfin's range (northern California to British Columbia) most of the soupfins were males. In the central California area a 50:50 ratio prevailed between the sexes, but in southern California females predominated.

From the standpoint of color the great blue shark *(Prionace glauca)* is well named. Its upper surface is a dark blue, almost indigo, which fades almost imperceptibly to a gleaming white on the undersurface. As in many other fishes, the beautiful color disappears soon after the fish dies. It has a sharp nose and very long pectoral fins, a slender body, and an elongate upper tail lobe with

31

Blue shark (Prionace glauca); Atlantic-Pacific marine.

a notch near the top. The great blue shark has been reported in both tropical and temperate waters around the world. Although several species have been described, most authorities recognize only one. The largest specimen ever captured measured 12 feet 7 inches and, like all blue sharks, was very slender. Blue sharks measuring as much as 9 feet in length weigh no more than 164 pounds. Females mature at a length of about 7 feet 6 inches. The maximum number of young recorded in a litter is 54, which was reported from the Mediterranean. In the Pacific, litters usually range from four to forty.

The American Atlantic lemon shark *(Negaprion brevirostris)* is one of the most common inshore species, and it ranges from North Carolina to Brazil.

It is occasionally found in brackish and even in fresh water. Its body usually has a yellowish tinge; hence the name. The upper surface may range from yellowish brown to bluish gray, and the undersurfaces may be white, yellow, or grayish olive. Besides the color, two characteristics help to identify this shark: a second dorsal fin which is almost as large as the first dorsal; and some very small teeth, usually one to three, found in the center of both the upper and lower jaws. These teeth are only about half the size of the rest and thus provide a conspicuous means of identification. Newborn lemon sharks are found from May to September and measure about 2 feet in length. Maturity is reached at about 7 feet 6 inches, and the maximum length is about 11 feet.

The silky shark *(Carcharhinus falciformis)* is very common offshore in both the Atlantic and the Pacific. Yet, strangely enough, it was not until 1953 that it was even tentatively identified from the Pacific. The silky shark is a member of the ridged-back group of carcharinid sharks; it has an obvious ridge down the center of the back between the first and second dorsal fins. The pectoral fins are extremely long, the eyes are small, and the second dorsal and anal fins have long, separate projections extending from their base.

The most common shark in the Atlantic and Pacific offshore waters is a gray shark that usually has whitish tips on the pectoral fins, on the first dorsal fin, and sometimes on the upper lobe of the tail fin. This oceanic whitetip shark *(C. longimanus)* is not to be confused with the whitetip of the Indian and Pacific oceans that has a similar pattern. Several features besides the color are useful in identification: long pectorals, a short snout, and a first dorsal fin that is broadly rounded at the top (most shark dorsals are somewhat pointed at the top). In addition, the rear tip of the anal fin is very long, extending to the small notch just in front of the tail fin. This species reaches a maximum length of about 13 feet.

There are two common Atlantic blacktips: a small species, *C. limbatus* (6 feet 6 inches), and a large species, the spinner shark *(C. maculipinnis)*. Both have the amazing habit of jumping into the air like porpoises; on occasion they have been observed to spin three times before dropping back into the water. The Atlantic blacktips may be found in deep water, but the common Pacific blacktip *(C. melanopterus)* is a species found in very shallow water.

For many years the dangerous Lake Nicaraguan shark was considered a distinct species. Now it is generally recognized as a fresh-water population of the common Atlantic and Pacific bull shark *(C. leucas)*, a species well known for its ability to move into fresh water. It has been taken as far inland as

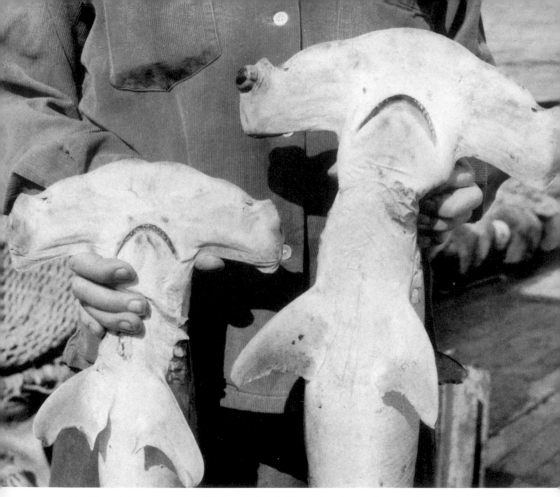

Scalloped hammerhead (Sphyrna lewini); Atlantic marine, and smooth hammerhead (S. zygaena); Atlantic-Pacific marine.

160 miles on the Atchafalaya River in Louisiana. Although the bull shark is considered dangerous, attack records are few. The same shark in Lake Nicaragua, however, does have a number of authenticated attacks attributed to it. The unresolved question is why the fresh-water habitat has changed the degree of aggressiveness of the species.

Hammerhead Sharks (Family Sphrynidae)

Large hammerhead sharks can be very aggressive and may be dangerous, especially to swimmers. The first human fatality credited to an American hammerhead was recorded about 1815 when the stomach of a big hammerhead captured off Long Island revealed portions of a human body. Records of unprovoked hammerhead attacks upon humans are also known from other parts of the world.

The hammerhead is one of the most readily identified of all sharks. The head is extended laterally in flattened, somewhat thickened "hammer-like" lobes; at the tips of these are located the eyes and nostrils. The distance between the eyes of a 15-foot hammerhead weighing 1,500 pounds may be as much as 36 inches. Scuba divers have described the startled reaction of a hammerhead when it first sees a diver: it tilts the hammers up and down alternately, perhaps trying to bring the eyes into better viewing position. In some species the individual hammer lobes may almost equal in length the width of the rest of the head, whereas in other sharks, such as the bonnethead, the lateral extensions of the hammer are much shorter, equal only to about one third of the width of the head.

"Shovelhead" is a much better name for the bonnet shark, since the head looks exactly like a spade with a rounded outer margin. These are small sharks, with a maximum length of 5 or 6 feet. Unlike the big hammerheads, they are not dangerous. The Atlantic bonnet or shovelhead *(Sphyrna tiburo)* is a very common shallow-water shark throughout most of its lengthy range from Brazil to Massachusetts. The same species is also thought to occur in the Pacific. Large hammerheads with extended hammers are usually found in deeper water than the bonnet sharks.

The hammerheads occur in all tropical seas and during summer periods may move northward or southward into temperate waters. The common hammerhead *(S. zygaena)* occurs on the African and European coasts of the Atlantic as well as on both the Atlantic and Pacific American coasts. The great hammerhead *(S. tudes)* is probably the largest species in the family, with many records of lengths up to 15 feet. Its range is like that of the common hammerhead.

There has been much speculation about the function of the hammer. One theory is that the extended hammers serve as balancers and make up to a certain extent for the lack of stabilizing keels along the sides of the tail as well as for the shortened pectoral fins.

Bullhead or Horn Sharks (Family Heterodontidae)

This family is a small but interesting group with only a single genus and fewer than ten species. The California species *(Heterodontus francisci)* is called the horn shark, whereas all the others are known as bullheads. These sharks do not occur in the Atlantic or the Mediterranean, although they are found throughout most of the other temperate and tropical waters of the world. The maximum length for all species is 4 feet 6 inches to 5 feet.

The mark of the bullhead and the horn shark is a large, blunt, heavy spine at the forward margin of each of the two dorsal fins. The dental plates curve upward from the upper jaws and downward from the lower jaws and are covered with many minute, sharp teeth. This peculiar mouth, together with the lateral nostrils, makes the shark appear piglike when seen from the front. The horn shark's egg is fluted and cylindrical with a spiral, shelflike rim around the outside; each female lays several eggs between the months of January and April. Incubation time is usually about seven months, and the newly hatched horn shark is about 8 inches in length.

Dogfishes (Family Squalidae)

The absence of the anal fin is the chief distinguishing characteristic of the dog-fishes. The family has two groups: the spiny dogs (47 species), so called because of the stout, sharp spine at the front edge of each dorsal fin, and the spineless dogs (8 species). The spineless dogs lack the spine in front of the second dorsal fin, and in most cases also lack the one in front of the first dorsal. For the most part, spineless dogs are sharks of deeper waters, ranging from 1,650 to 6,600 feet.

The common spiny dogfish *(Squalus acanthias)* has a gray body covered with small, indistinct white spots. It is primarily a temperate-water form, but it also ranges less commonly into arctic and tropical waters. It is abundant along the European coasts and on both the Atlantic and Pacific American coasts. A small venom gland hidden in a groove on the back of the spiny dog's dorsal spines can cause a painful injury. Other members of the family apparently do not have this venom gland.

Females of the common spiny dogfish reach a length of 4 feet and a weight of 20 pounds; the males are always smaller than the females. In Europe the dogfish is fished commercially and sold in the fresh-fish market; in the United States, however, it is not a profitable market item. During World War II, it was fished for the value of its liver, but with the development of synthetic vitamin A its value decreased and the fishery collapsed. Along the Atlantic coast, dogfishes have a seasonal migration pattern which is correlated with water temperature. They congregate in fast-moving schools, which make tremendous reductions in the local fish population and destroy a great deal of fishing gear.

While the common dogfish is an inshore and relatively shallow-water species, some of the other members of the family are strictly deep-water in habitat. This is true of the ten species of the genus *Etmopterus*, all of which have phosphorescent light organs along the sides of the body. This genus is of particular interest because it contains the smallest known shark, the Atlantic American *E. hillianus;* females of this species mature at a length of 12 inches and males at 10 inches. The largest specimen recorded measured less than 14 inches.

An unusual genus of spineless dogs is that of *Echinorhinus*, which includes two deep-water species found occasionally in American waters: the bramble shark from the Atlantic and the prickly shark from the Pacific. These are large, heavy-bodied sharks covered with small, spiny denticles.

Luminescent sharks are found only in deep water; one of the most brilliant is the pelagic deep-water dog, *Isistius brasiliensis*, from the tropical waters of the Atlantic, Pacific, and Indian oceans.

The largest of the spineless dogs belong to the genus *Somniosus;* the massive greenland shark *(S. microcephalus)* can reach a length of 21 feet and a weight of 2,250 pounds. Thirty gallons of liver oil can be obtained from a large individual. Its cousin, the Pacific sleeper shark *(S. pacificus)*, is a somewhat smaller species, reaching a length of 13 feet.

Angel Sharks (Family Squatinidae)

In many respects the angel shark is an evolutionary link, with some features that are sharklike and others that are skatelike or raylike. The broad, flattened head and trunk make the angel shark look as though it were a distant cousin of the skatelike guitarfish. Like the latter species, it has conspicuous spiracles, two small dorsal fins, and no anal fin; the mouth, however, is located at the anterior edge of the head. Unlike the skates or rays, it has nostrils just above the mouth, and each is equipped with two very conspicuous whiskers which extend into the entrance of the mouth. The profile of these whiskers is important in identifying the various species of angel sharks. The anterior edges of the large pectoral wings are not attached to the head as they are in the guitarfish. There are six to seven rows of heart valves, as in the skates or rays, but the gill openings are on the sides of the head rather than under the pectoral wings. The angel shark also has sharklike free eyelids and a typical sharklike motion when swimming.

With the exception of the European angel shark, which reaches 8 feet and a weight of 160 pounds, all of the other ten species in the single genus in the family rarely grow to more than 4 or 5 feet in length. The majority are inshore species and seldom stray into very deep water; there is a record, however, of a specimen of the Atlantic American *Squatina dumerili* from a depth of 4,200 feet. Some species move into shallow water to drop their young. Others show evidence of a yearly migration, the details of which are unknown. As indicated by the distribution of the Pacific American *Squatina californica*, which ranges from Alaska to Lower California, these sharks are principally temperate-water species.

Angel sharks are not dangerous to swimmers; out of the water, however, they have a very nasty disposition, as many an unwary fisherman can testify. The shark often swings its body from side to side if picked up by the tail, closing its jaws with resounding snaps of its dangerous, spikelike teeth. In captivity it commonly refuses to feed and thus may survive for only a few weeks or months.

SKATES AND RAYS (Order Rajiformes)

Several external features set the skates and rays apart from the other elasmobranchs. Their greatly enlarged pectoral fins are attached to the sides of the head, and the gills are on the undersides of these fins. To avoid mud and detritus, the bottom-dwelling skates and rays bring water in through the spiracles on top of the back and out through the gill chambers. In contrast, the manta rays, which do not live on the bottom, breathe like normal fishes. Skates and rays also lack the free upper eyelid of the shark. About 340 species of this order are known at the present time.

Electric Rays (Family Torpedinidae)

On San Francisco Bay the old Chinese fishermen tell you, "Pick up electric ray by tail—no trouble." If both your hands and the tail of the ray are dry, this is correct, since the large, paired electric organs are located in the wings, next to the head. More than 200 volts have been recorded from some of these fishes, although the majority produce no more than 75 or 80 volts, and some even less

Top: Lesser electric ray (Narcine brasiliensis); Atlantic marine.
Bottom: Banded guitarfish (Zapteryx exasperata); Pacific marine.

Electric ray (Narcine species); Pacific marine.

than 25 volts. As might be expected, the voltage drops radically with successive discharges. Several days are then required for the ray to recharge its "battery" and bring it up to normal strength.

Anatomically, the paired electric organs are composed of modified muscle tissue, and the cranial nerves supply the power to them. When discharging, the electric ray is positive on the upper surface and negative on the undersurface. By contrast, the electric eel is positive on the head and negative on the tail, whereas the electric catfish is just the reverse. These differences in polarity are due to differences in the arrangement of the electric plates, or disks.

The ability to discharge an electric current voluntarily can be useful to a fish in several ways. If the voltage and amperage are sufficient, the discharge can be used as a protective mechanism or as a kill pulse to stun overly active prey. If microvoltages are produced, they can serve as a method of orientation, helping the fish to avoid obstacles by means of disturbances in its electric field. In the electric rays the discharge is used both as a means of protection and as an aid in feeding. Sometimes the slightest provocation will produce an entire chain of electrical outbursts.

About eleven genera and 36 species of electric rays are recognized. They are found in all of the oceans of the world from tropical to temperate climates. In their normal habitat electric rays form a sparse population and usually do not occur in as tremendous numbers as some of the sharks and other rays.

The genus *Torpedo*, with its fourteen species, is the largest in the family. A typical *Torpedo* has a well-rounded disk with a fairly well-developed tail and tail fin. Like other members of the family it lacks the venom spine. Two small dorsal fins are present on the tail; some of the other genera of electric rays have a single dorsal fin or entirely lack this feature. The eyes are small, and in some species vestigial; other electric rays are totally blind. In vertical distribution, the electric rays are found from the intertidal zone into water as deep as 3,000 feet.

The largest species is probably the American Atlantic *Torpedo nobiliana*, which is known to reach a length of more than 5 feet and a weight of 160 or perhaps even 200 pounds. One of the smallest species is the beautifully patterned 18-inch lesser electric ray *(Narcine brasiliensis)*. It is found in very shallow water and ranges from North Carolina to Brazil. On the West Coast the Pacific electric ray *(T. californica)* has a more limited range, occurring from British Columbia to southern California. It reaches a modest size of about 4 feet and 90 pounds, and normally prefers water more than 100 feet deep.

Guitarfishes (Family Rhinobatidae)

The elongate body of the guitarfish is flattened along the sides of the head and trunk, with the pectorals extended as small raylike wings. The gills are on the underside of the pectoral fins. These fishes are found in tropical and temperate waters around the world. Many species travel in schools, sometimes in tremendous numbers. A length of 5 or 6 feet is the usual size for adults. The one exception is the giant Indo-Pacific *Rhynchobatos djiddensis*, which reaches a length of 10 feet and a weight of 500 pounds.

The guitarfishes are a shallow-water group that feed on the bottom and are often found in bays and estuaries. Small crustaceans are their preferred food items. Their grinding teeth are well adapted to this type of food supply, for they are very small, numerous, and arranged in as many as 65 or 70 rows. Guitarfishes are ovoviviparous, the young hatching from the eggs before they leave the body of the mother. Nine genera of guitarfishes are recognized. There are fifteen species in eight of these genera, and the remaining genus, *Rhinobatos*, includes at least thirty other species.

Most of the species of guitarfishes are similar in appearance; however, a few do show certain differences. The Atlantic guitarfish *(Rhinobatos lentiginosus)*, found from North Carolina to Yucatan, can easily be recognized by the numerous small whitish dots covering the upper surface of the body and tail. The Brazilian guitarfish *(R. horkelii)* is a nondescript brownish species common in many areas along the South American coast. Only a specialist could distinguish it from the American Pacific *R. productus*, which ranges from Monterey Bay south into the Gulf of California. The most attractive species is certainly the 3-foot dark-banded guitarfish *(Zapteryx exasperata)*, which ranges from San Diego southward.

Guitarfishes are usually the most docile of fishes. However, a diver in the La Jolla area who was free-diving for sand dollars recorded a strange experience. A male guitarfish attacked him, seizing the calf of his leg. The blunt, flat teeth did no more than dent the skin!

Sawfishes (Family Pristidae)

The sawfishes and saw sharks are invariably confusing since they are similar in appearance. As revealed by the gill openings located on the underside of the pectoral fins, the sawfish is a ray. By contrast, the saw sharks, of the family Pristiophoridae, have the gill openings on the sides of the body slightly above the pectoral fins. Saw sharks are not found in North American waters.

For all practical purposes, the sawfish is nothing more than an overgrown guitarfish with an ancient double-edged saw-toothed sword attached to its nose. These fishes are ovoviviparous, the young being born alive. Like the spines of unborn stingrays, the sawteeth are flexible until after birth; thus birth can take place without injury to the mother.

Sawfishes commonly occur in tropical salt and brackish waters around the world. In Florida's Indian River one fisherman captured more than 300 during a single season. They also migrate readily into fresh water; Lake Nicaragua, for example, has a well-established population.

Classification of the sawfishes is dependent upon the presence or absence of a lower lobe on the tail, the number of teeth along the sides of the saw or rostrum, and the position of the dorsal fins. The common sawfish of the western Atlantic,

Sawfish (Pristis pectinata); Atlantic marine.

Pristis pectinata, can easily be identified by the lack of a lower tail lobe and by the presence of 25 to 32 pairs of rostral teeth. The eastern Atlantic *P. pristis* has only 16 to 20 pairs of rostral teeth and also lacks the tail lobe.

The saw is a handy tool; it is used not only for digging up the sandy bottom, but also for clubbing prey. The sawfish swims rapidly through a school of fishes, flailing the saw from side to side, thus wounding or impaling many victims. It then cruises about, eating its prey at leisure. Despite the sawfish's fearful reputation among some native peoples, it is fairly docile in captivity, as shown by those at Marineland in California.

Skates (Family Rajidae)

The typical skate is a flat-bodied fish with a widely expanded pair of pectoral wings extending forward around the head as a thin, shelflike plate. In some species a nose or rostral cartilage provides support for a forward extension, giving the skate an extremely elongate nose. The eyes are usually conspicuously placed on top of the head, and the spiracles are immediately adjacent. The tail is slender and often short, and it has two small dorsal fins. The mouth and adjacent nostrils as well as the five paired gill openings are on the undersurface. The teeth are small, numerous, usually rounded, and arranged in several series. The skate's food is usually composed of bottom-dwelling invertebrates, although some of the European species seem to be quite adept at catching small fishes such as herring. Mature females are much larger than mature males; the latter may be distinguished by the presence of claspers attached to the inner surface of the ventral fins. Sometime after copulation the females deposit flattened, rectangular eggs encased in a leather-like protective sheath made of keratin. Each corner of the egg has a slender finger or tendril by which it often anchors itself to objects on the bottom.

Skates are found in most temperate and tropical seas and occasionally in brackish water, but are inexplicably absent from the Hawaiian Islands, Micronesia, and Polynesia, as well as from the northeastern coastal area of South America. They most frequently inhabit sand, gravel, or mud bottoms in shallow water at depths of less than 600 feet; there are, however, a few species such as the Pacific American *Raja abyssicola* that have been taken at depths as great as 7,200 feet. More than 100 species of skates have been described in the scientific journals, the majority of them assigned to the large genus *Raja*. Of the more than forty species along the American Atlantic coast, one of the most common is the little skate *(R. erinacea)* which ranges from South Carolina to Nova Scotia. When fully grown it is only about 20 inches long and weighs slightly more than a pound. By contrast, one of the larger species, the Pacific American big skate *(R. binoculata)*, has a maximum length of 8 feet.

Some skates have electric organs formed from modified musculature along the sides of the tail. The nerve supply to the electric organs of skates comes from the spinal nerves, whereas that of the electric rays (whose electric organs are located in the wings) is derived from the cranial nerves.

Stingrays (Family Dasyatidae)

The two principal families of rays, the dasyatid stingrays and the myliobatid eagle rays, have venom spines; usually a single flattened and tapered spine is attached to the dorsal surface of the tail. The two families can be easily distinguished by the fact that the wing fins of the stingrays extend around in front of the head as a thin, flattened shelf, whereas in the eagle rays this wing-fin extension forms a thick, fleshy lip. The stingray gets its fearful reputation from the many small, sharp teeth along the sides of this spine. In the dasyatid stingrays the tail is usually very slender and tapering, and in most species much longer than the body disk. Since the tail is very flexible, it can usually swing the hardened spine against objects in almost any direction. Some rays always switch the tail sideways, whereas others invariably throw it vertically forward toward the head.

Ichthyologists classify the dasyatid rays in five genera. *Dasyatis*, with some thirty species, is the largest genus, and it contains the biggest rays. All dasyatids possess the venom spine with the exception of the two species of the African genus *Urogymnus* and one Atlantic butterfly ray *(Gymnura micrura)*. Most of the species are restricted to saltwater, but a few occasionally migrate into brackish and fresh water; in South America, in fact, there are several stingrays that never leave fresh water. Most dasyatid stingrays are shallow-water forms, seldom going deeper than 360 feet.

The dasyatid stingrays range in size from mature round rays weighing only 1.5 pounds and measuring 12 inches across the wings to the giant Australian stingray weighing 750 pounds and measuring 6 to 7 feet across the wings. All dasyatids have powerful grinding teeth, which are small, numerous, and arranged in many rows. The stingray's normal food consists of any crustaceans, clams, or fish that are readily available. These are quickly sucked into the mouth and ground to pieces. The entire family is ovoviviparous; the female produces eggs that are hatched within her, and the young are born alive.

The venom glands of the stingray are usually located in paired grooves that run the length of the poison spine. When the membrane covering the spine is torn as a result of contact with a fishing net or some unsuspecting person's foot, the combined skin and venom glands of the fish are torn from the spine. The venom of the round stingray affects the human circulatory system. Its most serious effect is upon the heart muscle, producing an irregular beat or actual stoppage. It can also affect the respiratory, urinary, and central nervous systems. As far as is known, stingray wounds of the extremities alone have never been fatal, but abdominal wounds are more serious and can cause death.

The checklist of common names for United States and Canadian fishes shows eight Atlantic and four Pacific species. One of the most common is the 5-foot-wide southern stingray *(Dasyatis americana)*, which ranges from New Jersey to southeastern Brazil. Its cousin on the Pacific coast is the diamond stingray *(D. dipterura)*. In past years the Pacific round stingray *(Urolophus halleri)* has injured as many as five hundred swimmers per season on the bathing beaches of southern California. In the Atlantic a very similar species is the 14-inch-wide yellow stingray *(U. jamaicensis)*, which ranges from North Carolina to the northern coast of South America. Unlike its Pacific relative, it has not been a serious hazard to swimmers.

Eagle Rays (Family Myliobatidae)

A large fleshy pad extending around the front end of the head, giving the appearance of a flabby upper lip, is the mark of the eagle rays and their relatives, the bat rays and the cownose rays. In addition, the cownose rays *(Rhinoptera)* have the fleshy lobe divided into a right and a left portion.

The eagle rays and their cousins range widely throughout the tropical seas of the world, with a few species occurring in temperate and even cold waters. Generally they do not occur in large groups, although some species occasionally have dense populations. They are usually bottom-feeders.

With the exception of the three western Pacific duckbill rays (genus *Aetomyleus*), all of the other approximately 22 species in the family have the venom spine well developed; it is located just behind the dorsal fin and fairly far forward on the whiplike tail. As some of these rays reportedly reach a weight of 800 pounds and a length of 15 feet, the stinger can be a formidable weapon.

Pacific tropical stingray (Urolophus concentricus); Pacific marine.

Like the dasyatid rays, the eagle rays are noted for their heavy, flat teeth. Although it has never been tested, the grinding power of these molars must be tremendous, for they can easily crush the heaviest clamshells. Most of the genera have seven rows of teeth above and below, although several species of cownose rays are known to have nine rows. One genus, *Aetobatus*, has a single broad band of molars in each jaw. Almost any food item that gets in the way will usually find itself sucked into the eagle ray's powerful jaws. The eagle rays are ovoviviparous, and the young are born tail first, with the wings rolled up over the body like a double-rolled Mexican tortilla.

The peculiar bilobate fleshy pad around the front of the head resembling a split upper lip gives the cownose ray its name and also provides a quick method of identification. This feature and the presence in some of the species of eight or nine rows of grinding molar teeth are the principal characteristics that segregate the cownose from the rest of the eagle rays. The American cownose *(Rhinoptera bonasus)* occurs sporadically from New England to Brazil, but it is strangely absent from the Caribbean.

This species has a migration pattern that brings them northward to arrive in upper Chesapeake Bay about June 5 of each year. By September they have started to move southward again.

Like some of the other rays, the cownoses are great jumpers, occasionally leaping high in the air. Their maximum size across the wing tips is about 7 feet.

The spotted eagle ray *(Aetobatus narinari)* is one of the most beautiful of the large rays. The spots serve as an easy means of identification, as does the single band of teeth in each jaw. Although primarily an inshore species, the spotted eagle does have a worldwide distribution in tropical seas. The maximum width in the Atlantic is 7 feet 7 inches, but in South Africa it has a reported width of 11 feet.

The common bat stingray of the Pacific coast *(Myliobatis californica)* is noted for the maximum size difference between the adult males, 25 pounds, and the adult females, normally 160 pounds (with one record of 209 pounds). Males mature at 10 pounds and females at 52 pounds. In the past this species has been the scourge of the Pacific oyster industry, and protective fencing has been required to keep the bat rays out of the beds. The bat rays range from Oregon to the Gulf of California.

The genus *Myliobatis* has two additional widely distributed American Atlantic species, which are the bullnose ray *(M. freminvillei)* and the southern eagle ray *(M. goodei)*.

48   *Spotted eagle ray (Aetobatus narinari); Atlantic marine.*

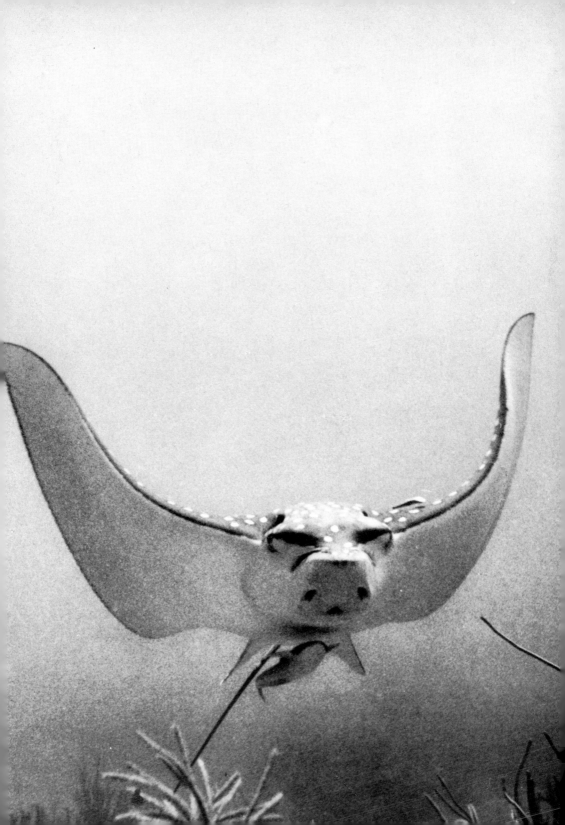

Bat stingray (Myliobatis californica); Pacific marine.

Mantas (Family Mobulidae)

The manta or devil ray is best described as an overgrown eagle ray that forsook feeding on the bottom for the more time-consuming feeding at the surface. A pair of slender feeding fins are useful in driving small crustaceans and other planktonic food into its mouth. These fins are attached on each side at the front of the head and are usually pointed forward. They fan the food toward the mouth as the giant ray cruises through swarms of prey in the area. The mantas are provided with a special gill-protecting mechanism located in the throat at the entrance to the gills. It is composed of a fine latticework of many-spined small protuberances that effectively hold the food in the mouth until it can be swallowed. At the same time, these strainers allow water to pass into the gills. Although the majority of rays respire by bringing water to the gills through the spiracles, it is suspected that the devil rays, like the bony fishes, bring water into the mouth and then into the gill cavity. Like the eagle rays, mantas are ovoviviparous. Ichthyologists are generally in agreement on a division of the family into four genera, based on whether the mouth is at the anterior end of the head or under the head as well as on the presence or absence of teeth. The genus *Ceratobatis* with its single species, *robertsi*, is known from one specimen from Jamaica. It is a unique genus in that the teeth are found only in the upper jaw. Members of the genus *Manta* have teeth in the lower jaw only. The remaining genera, *Mobula* and *Indomanta*, have teeth in both jaws, and the six species of *Mobula* are distinguished by having the mouth on the lower surface of the head. Among the mantas the poison tail spine may be present in one species of a genus and absent in another. For example, the common western Atlantic *Mobula hypostoma* lacks the spine, whereas the very similar but larger eastern Atlantic and Mediterranean *M. mobular* invariably has one or more spines.

In recent years several diving cinematographers have been able to record the peculiar back-circle movements in which the manta arches its back and does a continuous series of backdives lasting for several minutes. From the surface, the jumps that most of the mantas make on occasion are quite spectacular.

The checklist of common names shows five United States species with the giant 21-foot Atlantic and Pacific mantas heading the list for size, followed by the Atlantic devil ray and then two smaller Pacific species, the spinetail and the smoothtail mobulas.

CHIMAERAS (Order Chimaeriformes)

The chimaeras, sometimes called ratfishes, ghost sharks, or elephant fishes, have characteristics that in some respects appear to be intermediate between those of the sharks and the bony fishes. The chimaeras retain a cartilage skeleton like the sharks; they also lay eggs encased in horny capsules, and the males have paired claspers for internal fertilization. On the other hand, like the bony fishes they have a dermal opercle covering the four pairs of gill openings and an anal opening that does not empty into a cloaca but opens separately to the exterior just forward of the urogenital aperture. The chimaeras also have the upper jaw immovably fused to the cranium like the bony fishes. The most startling feature of this group of fishes is the presence of a unique special clasper just in front of the eyes on the head of the male. This is used by the male to hold the female's pectoral fin during mating. Another pair of male claspers is located in small pockets just forward of the pelvic fins. Empty pockets without claspers are sometimes present on females.

The entire group is a small one, containing three families and about 28 species. The families are easily segregated by the shape of the nose—rounded, pointed, or plow-shaped. For the most part the chimaeras are marine species living in deep water.

Short-nosed Chimaeras or Ratfishes (Family Chimaeridae)

The majority of the chimaeras belong to this family, which is distinguished by a rounded nose without an extension; this single feature completely segregates the seventeen species in this family from the other two families. The short-

Atlantic sturgeon (Acipenser oxyrhynchus); Atlantic marine and fresh-water, and shovelnose sturgeon (Scaphirhynchus platorynchus); fresh-water.

nosed chimaeroids have many distinctive characteristics. The circuitous mucous canals on the head are very prominent, as is the long poison spine at the front of the first dorsal fin. This venom spine is saw-toothed along its back edge, where a groove that contains the poison gland is located. The long, rodent-like tail is responsible for the name "ratfish." These fishes contain a liver oil that is highly prized as a lubricant for precision equipment.

The best-known American species is the 3-foot Pacific ratfish *(Hydrolagus colliei)*. It occurs offshore from Alaska to Baja California and is occasionally so abundant that fishermen may at times find their trawl nets entirely filled with these fish.

Bony Fishes *(Class Osteichthyes)*

Although the name "bony fishes" implies a skeleton of bone, the primitive members of this group still make use of the cartilage skeleton, and only the cranium is covered with dermal bones. The individual gill clefts of the sharks, skates, and rays are covered in the bony fishes by a single gill flap or opercle on each side. The paired claspers of the sharks and relatives are lacking, and fertilization of the eggs is usually external. In the few groups where fertilization is internal, there is a single copulatory organ modified from the anal fin. An air bladder or a primitive lung is usually present. In some of the more primitive bony fishes the shark-like spiral valve in the intestine is retained.

Sturgeons *(Family Acipenseridae)*

Ichthyologists consider the sturgeons and paddlefishes so closely related that they have merged them in a single order, the Acipenseriformes. This is the first and probably the most primitive of the bony fish orders.

The sturgeons are fishes of temperate waters and are found only in the Northern Hemisphere. Sturgeons are large fishes: many have been caught whose weights exceeded 2,000 pounds. Some species are found only in fresh water; others spend a portion of their lives in the ocean but return to fresh water to spawn. Their zoogeographic center is the region of central and eastern Europe extending into Asia. In this area there are about fifteen species of sturgeons, compared with only about nine species in North America.

In appearance, the sturgeon is an impressive, sharklike fish with a body that is scaleless except for five series of sharp-pointed, heavy, platelike scales along the sides. The turned-up tail and the spiracles which are found in some species add to the sharklike appearance.

In front of the underslung mouth, hanging down from the snout, are four long whiskers that work like a mine detector as the sturgeon moves slowly over the bottom. The sensitivity of the fleshy whiskers trailing in the sand makes up to some extent for the fish's poor eyesight. As soon as the whiskers pass over food, the protrusible mouth drops down with an elevator-like action, and the food is rapidly siphoned into the maw.

The sturgeon is one of the few fishes that are known to have taste buds outside of the mouth. The food it eats is small compared to its own size, so that in its normal habitat it must devote a great deal of time to foraging. For feeding, both the American lake sturgeon *(Acipenser fulvesens)* and the shovelnose sturgeon *(Scaphirhynchus platorynchus)* prefer a bottom of clear sand or gravel and adequate invertebrate life. Their food includes snails, crawfish, insect larvae, and such small fish as can be caught. The food supply of the ocean-going sturgeon is chiefly small invertebrates, many of which live on a mud bottom rather than on the clear bottom favored for feeding by the landlocked American species.

The largest American species, and incidentally the largest American freshwater fish, is the Pacific coast white sturgeon *(A. transmontanus)*. There is an unverified 1897 record of a British Columbia female weighing about 1,800 pounds. The next largest female recorded weighed 1,285 pounds and was caught in Vancouver, Washington, in June, 1912. In recent years, however, the largest individuals have usually weighed less than 300 pounds. The other American Pacific species, the green sturgeon *(A. medirostris)*, is found more often in brackish water and saltwater than is the white sturgeon. Its recorded maximum weight is 350 pounds, with a maximum length of 7 feet.

The eastern American lake or rock sturgeon has been known to reach a weight of 300 pounds and a length of 8 feet, whereas the shovelnose or hackleback rarely reaches a weight of 6 pounds and a length of 3 feet. Of the marine sturgeons, the American Atlantic *A. oxyrhynchus* reaches a maximum of 14 feet and 811 pounds. The largest sturgeon of all is the giant beluga *(Huso huso)* from the Caspian and Black seas and the Volga River. The record for this species is 14 feet and 3,000 pounds.

Significant reductions in the sturgeon population can result from only moderate fishing. Although large females sometimes produce as many as 2,500,000 to 5,000,000 eggs, there are indications that sexual maturity is not achieved in some species until the female reaches an age of about twenty years and a length of some 4 feet. It is therefore obvious that the loss, through fishing, of the large adults would result in a rapid decrease in reproductive potential. The incubation period of the fertilized egg is influenced not only by the species of sturgeon but also by the temperature of the water; hatching may take place any time from two weeks to almost three months.

Sturgeon roe or eggs is the principal source of caviar, though caviar can also be processed from the roe or eggs of many other kinds of fishes. Originally this epicurean delicacy came from several species of sturgeons in the Caspian and Black Seas and Volga River area of eastern Europe. Later, caviar production

Paddlefish (Polyodon spathula); fresh-water.

spread to western Europe, and within the past hundred years to the United States. Isinglass is another by product of the sturgeon fisheries; it is a transparent, almost-pure gelatin made from the air bladders of fishes, which has at times been more valuable than caviar.

Paddlefishes (Family Polyodontidae)

There are only two kinds of paddlefishes, one in the Yangtze River valley *(Psephurus gladius)* and the other in the Mississippi River valley *(Polyodon spathula)*. Together they make up a strange family of cartilaginous-bony fishes, the Polyodontidae.

On examining a paddlefish it is easy to see why it has occasionally been described as a new species of shark. However, the monstrous paddle attached

56

to its nose immediately challenges this identification. Although there is one shark, the deep-sea goblin, that has a paddle-like extension on its nose, this is quite small compared with that of the paddlefish, which is equal to about one third of the length of the fish. Under the paddle there are four very small barbels suggestive of the sturgeon family. The body of the paddlefish is smooth and scaleless. A cartilaginous skeleton supporting the body and a sharklike spiral valve in the intestine are among the primitive features of this archaic fish.

Capture of larval paddlefishes less than an inch in length is a rarity. By the time the fish has grown to $1^3/_8$ inches the nose has changed from an insignificant bump to a respectable beak, or rostrum, equal to one sixth of the total length. An adult paddlefish measuring 6 feet would have a paddle 4 inches wide and about 24 inches long, as measured from the upper edge of the mouth. Instead of probing with its paddle, the paddlefish catches its food by swimming about with its mouth wide open. Small crustaceans and planktonic organisms are strained from the water by the long gill rakers on the inner sides of the gills. The average adult American paddlefish found today weighs from 30 to 50 pounds, and the largest recorded specimen weighed 168 pounds and measured slightly more than 6 feet.

Alligator gars (Lepisosteus spatula); fresh-water.

The original distribution of the American paddlefish was over most of the Mississippi valley and from North Dakota to New York and down to South Carolina. Because of dams, pollution, and many other factors, it is now greatly restricted in its range and is abundant only in certain limited areas.

Gars (Family Lepisosteidae)

Many a skin diver in fresh water has aimed his spear at a gar only to see the weapon ricochet from the fish's heavy external armor. Close examination of this formidable protective covering reveals that it is composed of scales arranged in rhombic- or diamond-shaped flat plates which do not overlap like normal fish scales. In addition, these plates are covered with a substance different from that of normal fish scales, and have a different method of growth. The result is a sturdy outer layer which is difficult to penetrate.

Gars are usually found in shallow, weedy areas. Much of the time they show little movement and appear to be suspended in mid-water. However, they can move extremely fast, especially when chasing food. Gars are generally not used for food, although the Seminole Indians in the Florida Everglades include them in their diet. The giant tropical gar *(Lepisosteus tristoechus)*, which grows to lengths of 10 and perhaps 12 feet, is reported to be a food fish in the markets of Tampico, Mexico. Gar scales have some use in making ornaments and jewelry.

The vertebrae of gars are clearly reptilian in nature. Most fishes have vertebrae that are concave at both ends, but gars have ball-and-socket joints, with the anterior end of each vertebra being convex and the posterior end concave. Both the anal and dorsal fins lack spines and have fewer than a dozen rays each; these two fins are located far back on the body, just before the heterocercal tail.

About eight species of gars are recognized. They are limited to North America from southeastern Canada to Costa Rica, and do not occur west of the Rocky Mountains. Although primarily a fresh-water family, some, such as the two or three species of alligator gars, do move into saltwater. The most widely distributed member of the family is the longnose gar *(L. osseus);* it ranges from the Mississippi basin eastward through all of the seaboard states. The length of the jaws in front of the eyes is about three times the length of the head behind the eyes. Other species of gars have much shorter jaws, usually no longer than twice the distance from the eye to the opercle, at the end of the head.

Bowfin (Amia calva); fresh-water.

The shortnose gar *(L. platostomus)* lacks the mottled color pattern of its cousin, the otherwise very similar spotted gar *(L. productus)*. The largest lepisosteid ever caught in the United States was an alligator gar *(L. spatula)* that weighed 302 pounds and measured almost 10 feet. This species has the most limited distribution of all the gars, being restricted mainly to the southern states.

Because of their unique characters the gars are placed in a separate order, the Semionotiformes.

Bowfin (Family Amiidae)

In ancient times the bowfin *(Amia calva)* was widely distributed through the fresh waters of North America, but it is now restricted to the waters of the eastern United States. A variety of names has been applied to it, such as dog-fish, grindle, spot, and mudfish. It is an easy fish to identify because of the long, spineless dorsal fin (with about 58 rays) that runs from the forward part of the back down to the base of the tail. On the upper part of the caudal peduncle just in front of the tail there is usually a large dark spot. Males have this spot edged with orange or yellow, but the females lack the edging, and sometimes the spot will be missing. On the underside of the head between the two lower jawbones is a large and distinctive gular plate. The head is covered with bony plates and the rest of the body with heavy scales. The tail is basically lopsided, although externally it appears symmetrical.

Internally there is a vestige of the primitive spiral valve of the sharks and rays, and the well-developed air bladder has a vascular internal surface so that it can act as a lung. This enables the bowfin to live in water almost devoid of oxygen or to survive out of water for as long as 24 hours. Large bowfins may reach a length of 3 feet and a weight of more than 8 pounds, although the usual maximum length is around 2 feet.

Since bowfins eat all kinds of fishes and invertebrates, in some areas where they are extremely abundant measures have been taken to wipe them out. In some parts of the South they are used for food, but in the North they are considered trash fish. Their preferred spawning sites are weedy areas along the margins of lakes and streams. The male bowfin not only builds the nest, but also guards it after the female lays her eggs and chaperones the youngsters for a short time after they are hatched. Like lungfishes and sturgeons, the newly hatched bowfin has an adhesive organ on the snout that enables it to attach itself to aquatic vegetation. Growth is rapid; a year-old bowfin may be 5 to 9 inches long.

Ichthyologists place the bowfins in a separate order—the Amiiformes.

Tarpons (Family Elopidae)

The fishes of the elopid family all have a long, deeply forked tail and, near the center of the body and more or less opposite the ventral fins, a single dorsal fin of soft rays. The tarpon and the ladyfish sometimes called the tenpounder have a distinguishing character that other fishes of this group lack: a fairly large, bony gular plate located under the mouth, between the two mandibles. They also have many sharp, small teeth. Although primarily marine, the elopids are also known from brackish and even fresh waters.

The larval forms of the elopids are similar to those of the albulids, or bonefishes—that is, bandlike and transparent—and they shrink radically in length at the time of metamorphosis into the juvenile stage. Because of these special characteristics, the elopids and albulids are set aside in their own order, the Elopiformes.

The tarpons *(Megalops)* have the last ray of the dorsal extended as a long filament. Because of its explosive reaction to being hooked, the Atlantic tarpon *(M. atlantica)* has long been known as one of the most spectacular game fishes. The record is a giant 8-foot individual that weighed an estimated 340 pounds. In the summertime the Atlantic tarpon ranges as far north as Cape Cod, but it is most abundant in tropical areas. The Pacific tarpon *(M. cyprinoides)* is a much smaller species than its Atlantic cousin, seldom growing as long as 40 inches. It ranges from Africa through the Indian and Pacific oceans to Guam. Unfortunately, neither the tarpons nor the ladyfishes are good-tasting food fishes, although they are sometimes eaten.

There is probably only a single species of ladyfish *(Elops saurus)*, although as many as seven have been described, including the Pacific form, the machete *(E. affinis)*. Ladyfish occur around the world in tropical and subtropical seas, reaching a length of 3 feet and a weight of 30 pounds.

Bonefishes *(Family Albulidae)*

Ichthyologists find the bonefish interesting because of its unusual larval stage. The leptocephalus larva, as it is called, is in many respects similar to that of the eels. Two species of bonefishes are recognized: *Albula vulpes*, which is cosmopolitan in shallow, warm, marine waters, and *Dixonina nemoptera*, which is found only in the West Indies. The latter differs from *Albula* in that the last ray of both the dorsal and anal fins is modified as a long, extended filament. Thick transparent cartilage covers the pointed head of the albulids, and the mouth recedes. The teeth are numerous, small, blunt, and rounded. The dorsal fin with its ten to fourteen soft rays is in the center of the body opposite the ventrals, and the caudal fin is deeply forked. Adult bonefishes range in size up to about 3 feet 6 inches, with a maximum weight of 18 pounds. Although they are sometimes sold in markets, they have many small, fine bones which limit the ways in which they can be prepared for the table.

EELS *(Order Anguilliformes)*

With the exception of one family of fresh-water eels, all of the members of this order—at least 22 families and perhaps 350 species—are marine in habitat, the majority living in shallow water. All eels have several features in common. They lack the pelvic or ventral fins, and the dorsal and anal fins are usually continuous with the tail fin. The air bladder has an open duct to the throat. Except for about three of the 22 families, all of the eels lack scales. Most of them have a strange, transparent, ribbon-like larval form known as a lepto-cephalus. Because this larva is so radically different from the adult, many leptocephali have been described but not identified with the corresponding adults. At the time of metamorphosis, the leptocephalus, which usually measures from 2 to 8 inches in length, shrinks in size and gradually changes to a juvenile eel smaller than its leptocephalus stage. Although most of the eel-like species of fishes are placed in this single order, it is possible that when our knowledge is more complete, several orders will be recognized. As a group, eels are usually more active at night than in the daytime.

Fresh-water Eels (Family Anguillidae)

The anguillid eels live in a variety of fresh-water habitats such as streams, rivers, ponds, and lakes; at spawning season they return to saltwater. Although none is found in the eastern Pacific or south Atlantic, about sixteen species are recognized. The anguillids differ from most of the other eel families in the pos-session of scales, in this case of the embedded cycloid type that are visible only on careful inspection. Externally, the fresh-water eels and the conger eels are confusingly similar in appearance. They may be distinguished, however, by the position of the dorsal fin, which begins just behind the pectoral fin in the congers and at a considerable distance behind the pectoral in the anguillids.

The two North Atlantic species, the European *Anguilla anguilla*, and the American *A. rostrata* have similar life histories. The American eel has limited commercial use, but the European eels have been the basis of valuable fisheries for centuries. To understand the American fresh-water eel, it is helpful to begin with the European species, which was the first to be studied in detail.

When the females of the European eels are twelve years old and about 5 feet long, they migrate back to salt water; the males, however, start their migration from fresh to salt water when they are four to eight years old and a length of about 20 inches. At this time the eels change from yellow to silver in color, and since they are quite fat, their value as food is at its peak. Instinctively, the adult eels head for the Sargasso Sea, a tropical water area of pelagic marine plants ex-tending for many miles in the region around Bermuda. When the eels finally reach their destination a year later, having traveled 3,000 miles without food, they spawn at a depth of 1,500 feet, where the water is saltier than it is in any other part of the Atlantic. The adults die after spawning and the eggs float to the surface, where they soon hatch into leptocephali. These larvae then start on the return trip, which requires three years. During this time they metamorphose, becoming young elvers of about 3 inches by the time they reach the European streams and rivers.

The American eel *(A. rostrata)* spawns in almost the same area of the ocean as the European eel; however, the leptocephalus requires only a single year to reach the American coasts in contrast to the three years required for the European species. The American range is from Greenland to Labrador, southward to the Gulf of Mexico and perhaps even Brazil, and as far inland as most of the mid-central states.

The blood of the fresh-water eel contains a powerful neurotoxin that causes serious infection if it gets into a human cut or wound. This can happen when the eel is being prepared for market.

Spaghetti or Worm Eels (Family Moringuidae)

The spaghetti eels form a small tropical family of about twenty species. Since there is a considerable difference between the sexes, it is probable that this number will be substantially modified with future study. All moringuids have small pectoral fins, and some are known to be head burrowers. The typical spaghetti eel looks like a very elongated worm, often with one lip greatly overlapping the other. In some species it is thought that with maturity there is also a change from the habit of burrowing in the sand in shallow areas to a pelagic mode of life. The 20-inch adult Bahaman *Moringua edwardsi* is most often collected around lights at night; immature individuals do not seem to be attracted by light.

Moray Eels (Family Muraenidae)

For anyone living along a temperate or tropical coastline, the word "eel" invariably brings to mind the vicious moray. This is not surprising, for the morays are the commonest of the rock- and reef-dwelling tropical eels, not only in abundance but also in the number of different species. Most morays reach a maximum length of 4 or 5 feet, but there are occasional records of giants

63

measuring as much as 10 feet. Morays are regularly eaten by man in many parts of the world, although at least five species have been reported to be poisonous, with death resulting in about 10 per cent of the recorded cases. The muraenids are identified by a combination of characteristics, the most important being the absence of pectoral fins, dentition, color pattern, and the profile of the nostrils. They are also suspected of lacking the leptocephalus larval stage. About twelve genera and at least eighty species are recognized.

Although many of the morays are unicolored, such as the beautiful Atlantic *Gymnothorax funebris*, there are others that have picturesque patterns like that of the Atlantic blackedge moray *(G. nigromarginatus)*. Brilliant banded patterns are commonplace in the genus *Echidna*, the members of which also have a modified type of dentition, with flattened grinding teeth.

Eels benefit from a cleaning service provided by certain fishes and invertebrates that remove parasites from other larger fishes. Many eels are known to make periodic trips to the areas where these cleaners reside in order to have these helpful invertebrates and fish provide sanitation services for them. Despite the fact that most of these cleaners could be eaten at one gulp, the larger fishes seem to recognize their value and do not harm them.

Conger Eels (Family Congridae)

The congers usually have pectoral fins and are light-colored with a black band around the edge of the dorsal and anal fins. The dorsal fin begins just behind the pectoral fins, a feature that differentiates the conger from the similar freshwater eel; in the latter species the dorsal fin begins at a considerable distance from the pectorals. When the conger moves it presents a symphony of motion, as undulating ripples pass down the fins. Although congers are often found in shallow water, it is suspected that some of them require the pressure of deeper water to spawn and that they probably die after spawning. There are many genera and perhaps 100 species of congers, with some ranging in length to 6 or even 10 feet. The larger species are used as food in Europe and Japan.

In the past few years considerable interest engendered by diving biologists has centered on the tropical marine garden eels (subfamily Heterocongrinae). No more than eight or ten species are recognized; all are very slender, about the diameter of a pencil, and are usually 3 to 4 feet in length. Dense garden eel beds are often located on protected sandy bottoms that have enough current to bring in the necessary microplankton. As a diver approaches, the eels sink down

Moray eel (Gymnothorax species) and banded cleaner fish; Pacific marine.

into their holes, while at other times during the day they may extend the body vertically for 8 to 16 inches. In 1965 in the Gulf of California we captured our first living eels by use of quinaldine, a fish anesthetic. In laboratory and corridor display tanks we found them to be reasonably hardy, adapting readily to the constant tapping on the glass by visitors.

The knifetooth eels, placed by some investigators in the family Muraenesocidae, are included by others in the congrid family. About seventeen species of knifetooths are recognized, all characterized by a sharp row of large median teeth along the roof of the upper jaw. The silver conger *(Hoplunnis macrurus)* is an inshore species found from the northern to southwestern Gulf of Mexico.

Snake Eels *(Family Ophichthidae)*

The snake eels are tail burrowers and accordingly have very sharp, strong, spikelike tails. Although the majority of snake eels lack pectoral fins, a few do have very small pectorals. Typically, the dorsal fin starts just behind the head and extends for the full length of the body; the anal fin is much shorter. Ophichthid eels have a special nostril arrangement with the posterior nostril lying within or piercing the upper lip. Most snake eels are very slender and usually small, measuring less than 3 feet, although a few species may reach 5 or 6 feet. Distribution is worldwide, mostly in shallow tropical seas; the group is less abundant in more temperate waters. Brilliant banded and spotted patterns are prevalent in this family of more than 200 species. There are 27 species in United States and Canadian waters, 24 in the Atlantic, and three in the Pacific.

Herrings *(Family Clupeidae)*

A small school of sardines or herrings moves through the water as a single unit. In the Northern Hemisphere they school mainly in a counterclockwise direction, whereas their cousins in the Southern Hemisphere are said to school clockwise. Most of the clupeids are less than 18 inches in length, but there are a few larger ones, such as the American shad, which may reach 30 inches. Commercially, the herrings, sardines, and their relatives form one of the world's most important groups of food fishes. Family identification of these fish is fairly simple, since most of the approximately 190 species and 50 genera are similar in appearance. Identification of individual species, however, is another matter, since even the specialists are not in agreement about all of them.

Garden eels (Taenioconger digueti); Pacific marine.

All of the clupeids are noted for their oily flesh. The body itself is deeply
compressed laterally and covered with deciduous scales, which form a knifelike
ridge along the center line of the undersurface of the body. The presence of
this sharp ridge means that the fish belongs to the main clupeid herring group
while its absence indicates the round herring group, which has been recognized
as a separate family, the Dussumieriidae. In all herrings the dorsal fin is placed
near the center of the body, the adipose fin is missing, and the tail fin is deeply
forked. The large, usually toothless mouth works like a siphon to suck in small
planktonic organisms which are caught on the gill rakers in the throat. Although
the majority of clupeids are primarily marine, many move easily into brackish
and fresh water. Considering the combined species, the optimum temperature

Overleaf: Dwarf herring (Jenkinsia lamprotaenia); Atlantic marine.

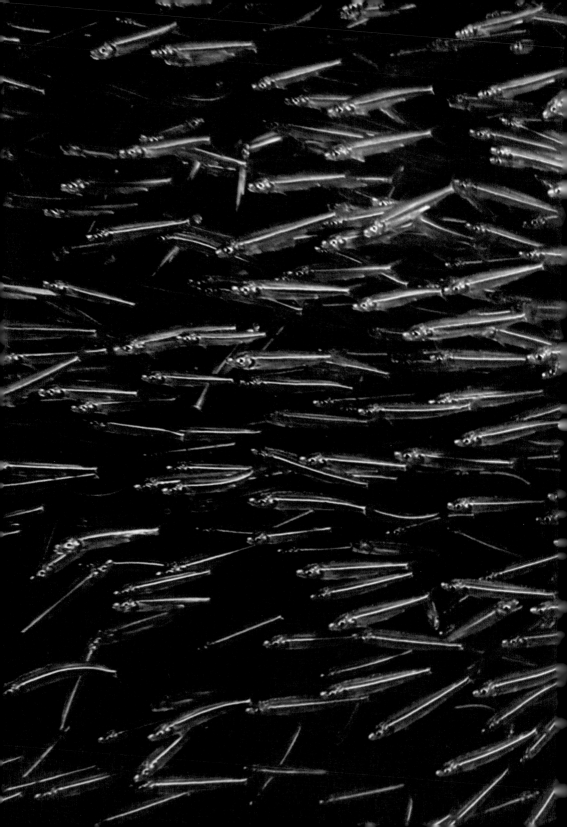

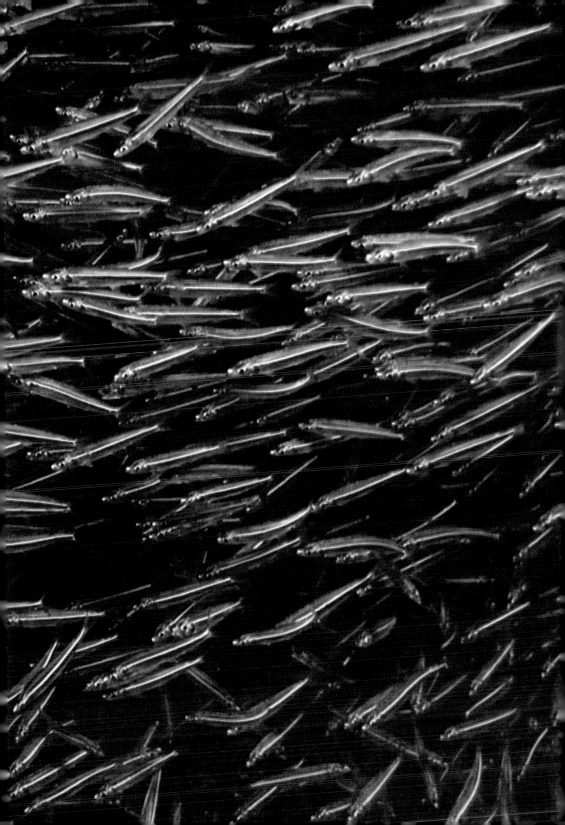

range is wide—from the warmest water in the tropics to very cold water in the far north, depending on the species.

Spawning activity shows a great deal of variation among the clupeids. The Pacific American sardine *(Sardinops sagax)* spawns offshore during the spring and summer months and has surface-floating eggs. whereas others, such as the American shad *(Alosa sapidissima)*, migrate into rivers, spawning in fresh-water. The Pacific herring *(Clupea pallasi)* moves into shallow-water bays at spawning time, depositing the eggs on seaweeds and other suitable surfaces. The Atlantic herring *(C. harengus)* is also a bottom spawner, leaving its eggs attached to shells and weeds of various types. It does not necessarily move into shallow water to spawn, however, as we know from eggs that have been brought up from as deep as 80 feet.

Other important members of the clupeid family include the American menhaden *(Brevoortia tyrannus)*, which, although not a food fish, is used extensively to manufacture fish meal. The alewife *(Pomolobus pseudoharengus)* is found not only in marine waters from Nova Scotia to Florida but has also moved inland into the fresh waters of all the Atlantic seaboard states. The thread herring *(Opisthonema oglinum)* is a Caribbean species that sometimes appears northward along the Atlantic coastline. It has a characteristically long, threadlike extension of the last fin rays of the dorsal.

As for the round herrings, fewer than fifteen species divided into four genera are recognized. The majority of species are tropical marine in habitat and do not occur in vast schools like some of the clupeid herrings. Probably the most abundant round herrings are two species of small, slender, silvery fishes belonging to the genus *Spratelloides*. Whenever one hangs a night light over the side of a ship throughout the tropical areas of the Indian and Pacific oceans, these fishes move into the lighted area in tremendous swarms. Although they measure no more than 4 inches in maximum length, they are harvested commercially in some areas and made into a tasty fish paste.

Gizzard herrings are similar to round herrings in that they too have in the past been given family status. These fishes derive their name from the peculiar muscular stomach which the approximately half-dozen species in the group possess. Externally they look like threadfin herrings, being very deep-bodied and having a sharp ridge along the abdomen and the last rays of the dorsal fin extended as a long filament. The Atlantic gizzard shad *(Dorosoma cepedianum)*, which reaches a length of 20 inches, has been widely introduced as a forage fish into many areas of the central and eastern United States.

Anchovies (Family Engraulidae)

The mouth of the anchovy is set far back on the underside of the head, and the lower jaw is small and inconspicuous, so the fish appears to be chinless. This characteristic instantly enables one to recognize any of the over 100 species in the family. Except for the chin, the anchovy looks much like a small round herring. The single dorsal fin is almost at the center of the body, and the tail fin is deeply notched. The adipose fin and lateral line are absent. The anchovies are small fishes that are always found in schools. The majority of them are less than 5 inches in length, with a very few growing as large as 9 inches.

Anchovies are economically valuable as food for human consumption and as live and frozen bait for fishermen. Their greatest abundance is in tropical marine waters. About 125 species are recognized, with almost ninety being found in the Americas. The 6-inch striped anchovy *(Anchoa hepsetus)* is one of the common Atlantic species, ranging from Chesapeake Bay to Uruguay. The anchoveta *(Cetengraulis mysticetus)*, a wide-ranging species found from southern California to Peru, is a smaller species and is in much demand as live bait by tuna fishermen. Most of the fishing by tuna clippers for this bait is carried on in Mexican and Central American waters. The northern anchovy *(Engraulis mordax)*, a large species ranging from British Columbia to the tip of Baja California, is one of the most important Pacific members of the family. It reaches a length of about 9 inches.

Mooneyes (Family Hiodontidae)

The two species of mooneyes are the central and eastern North American representatives of an ancient group known as the osteoglossiform fishes. The mooneye, sometimes called toothed herring *(Hiodon tergisus)*, is characterized by very large eyes and a silvery color; it reaches a length of 17 inches and a weight of 2.5 pounds. It is usually found in clear water and is a good game fish but not a palatable food item. The goldeye *(H. alosoides)* is similar to the mooneye in general appearance but is dark blue above and silvery on the sides, with a slight touch of golden color on the eyes. It may be distinguished from the mooneye by the sharp ridge along the underside of the belly in front of the ventral fins. Its maximum size is around 20 inches and it has a weight of slightly more than 2 pounds. Unlike the mooneye, the goldeye will tolerate muddy and turbid water.

Northern anchovies (Engraulis mordax); Pacific marine.

TROUT, SALMON, PIKES, MUDMINNOWS AND THEIR RELATIVES (Order Salmoniformes)

This large order contains eight suborders made up of some 37 families of which we shall discuss 10. In addition to the well-known trout, salmon, whitefishes, grayling, pikes, mudminnows and lizardfishes, there are some 28 families of deep-sea fishes. All members of this group have soft fin rays, and some have a small adipose fin on the back just ahead of the tail.

Trout, Salmon, Whitefishes and Grayling (Family Salmonidae)

The salmonids are a small family, but they include some of the world's greatest sport fishes. They have one identification mark in common—a small, fleshy adipose fin on the dorsal surface of the body opposite the anal fin. Although these fishes were originally limited to the Northern Hemisphere, they have been introduced successfully into many parts of the Southern Hemisphere.

Trout are usually restricted to fresh water, but there are a few types, such as the steelhead, that regularly migrate to the ocean between spawnings, and a number of other species that may do so under conditions favorable to migration. Many popular articles and books on the salmon have made its life history well known: typically, it spends most of its adult life in the ocean, returning to the fresh water where it was hatched only to spawn and die. There are, however, exceptions to this rule; landlocked, fresh-water salmon, such as the kokanee *(Oncorhynchus nerka kennerlyi)*, a type of Pacific sockeye, obviously cannot make the trip to the ocean. The Atlantic salmon *(Salmo salar)*, which is actually a type of steelhead, or ocean-run trout, also has landlocked populations, such as the sebago, in some of the eastern North American lakes as well as other populations in some of the European lakes.

Details of spawning vary with the species, but usually the spawners move upstream in the spring or occasionally in the autumn. Sometimes they must fight their way against tremendous obstacles, and even jump falls, until they can find a suitable gravel bottom that can be excavated by the female. Although most trout and salmon are stream spawners, there are at least two species, the brook trout *(Salvelinus fontinalis)* and the lake trout *(S. namaycush)*, that use the gravel beds of their home lakes for spawning. Having dug a depression in the gravel, the female pours the eggs into it, and at almost the same moment the male covers the eggs with milt. Finally, the female brushes gravel over the eggs so that they are protected from predators as well as from being washed downstream. Several of these spawning pockets may be filled with eggs before a pair have completed their reproductive functions. If the spawning pair are Pacific salmon, they soon die, but if they are trout, they may spawn for a number of years. Upon hatching, the larval trout or salmon has a large bulbous abdomen containing the egg sac, which provides the fry with its necessary food for the first few weeks of life. The larval salmonid usually stays in the gravel until the egg sac is absorbed, then works its way upward to become free-swimming.

Since trout and salmon eggs in the "eyed" stage (when the eyes first show) can be shipped without difficulty, these fishes have been widely distributed all over the world; therefore, the present distribution of any given species may bear little relationship to its original range. For example, the European brown trout *(Salmo trutta)* was brought into North America many years ago by fish culturists, and since then it has been widely planted over the continent in almost every area having suitable waters.

Because of the large pair of horizontal streaks, or cut marks, under the throat, the cutthroat trout *(S. clarki)* is one of the most spectacular of the salmonids. Its normal range is western North America. The char or brook trout *(Salvelinus fontinalis)* of eastern North America, and, through introduction, Europe, has a mottled pattern, usually with red spots on the sides. Identification can usually be made by the distinct white border along the anterior margins of the ventral and anal fins. Sea-run forms of the brook trout are present in some of the northern areas, for example along the Canadian coasts. In western North America the brook trout is replaced by another of the same genus, the Dolly Varden trout *(S. malma)*, which ranges from Alaska to the McCloud River in California.

The rainbow trout *(Salmo gairdneri)* and its several subspecies are highly popular with western American sportsmen. The brilliant reddish longitudinal stripe along the side of the body is the principal identification mark. The rainbow has an important ocean-run form popularly known as the steelhead and recognized technically under the name *S. gairdneri gairdneri*. It is usually less conspicuously banded than the fresh-water rainbow, and its black spots are more evident. The golden trout *(S. aguabonita)* is the high-mountain trout of western North America; it is seldom found at elevations of less than 8,000 feet. As an adult it retains its parr marks, the vertical bars found on the sides of all juvenile trout.

Of the seven species of Pacific salmon grouped together in the genus *Oncorhynchus*, five occur on the American coastline from Alaska to California. These are larger fishes than the trout, with some, such as the chinook salmon *(O. tshawytscha)*, reaching a weight of as much as 100 pounds.

All of the Pacific salmon are anadromous, that is they live in the ocean as adults but return to the stream in which they were hatched to spawn and then die. As mentioned, the Atlantic salmon is actually a sea-run trout; it does not die after the first spawning.

There is a considerable difference in the life histories of the various species of salmon. For example, the newly hatched fry of both the pink and the chum salmon migrate to the ocean soon after they are hatched; whereas those of the coho, chinook, and sockeye remain in the stream for as long as 12 to 36 months. Time spent in the ocean is also variable, with the pinks coming back to fresh water to spawn in the second year, cohos in the third year, chums mostly in the fourth year, and chinooks and sockeyes ranging between three and eight years. Two events in experiments with the salmon have been of great interest. First is the work of Dr. Lauren Donaldson at the University of Washington, who developed chum salmon that returned to spawn earlier in their third year and at a much larger size. He has also accomplished this for the steelhead. The second event was the introduction in 1966 of coho salmon into Lake Michigan. A sizable run later developed there, much to the delight of sport fishermen. The fishes average 11.5 pounds.

74   *Grayling (Thymallus arcticus); fresh-water.*

The whitefishes have sometimes been recognized as a separate family, the Coregonidae. They are closely related to the trout and salmon but have weaker mouths with few or no teeth, larger scales, and a very dull, silvery appearance. They have adipose fins, and are Northern Hemisphere species ranging from Arctic waters southward. From the standpoint of food value to man, they are undoubtedly one of the most important fresh-water groups. Whitefishes usually spawn in the fall, and always in fresh water, where the majority live. Several whitefishes of the genus *Coregonus* are known by the common name "cisco": for example, the blackfish cisco *(C. nigripinnis)* and the least cisco *(C. sardinella)*. In recent years sport fishermen have made use of the talents of northern bush pilots who fly to isolated areas where the fighting sheefish, or inconnu *(Stenodus leucichthys)*, abounds. This is one of the few whitefishes that moves readily into brackish water. It may reach a length of 59 inches and a weight of 63 pounds.

The grayling, with its long and beautiful flaglike dorsal fin, is prized both as a food fish and as a sport fish. Like the trout and salmon, the grayling has a small adipose fin, but it has a very small mouth, and fewer and larger scales along the sides of the body. It is entirely restricted to fresh water.

Graylings occur in the northernmost parts of both North America and Eurasia. Several species have been described, *Thymallus thymallus* being the common European species, and *T. arcticus* the North American form. The latter is found as far south as the southern limits of Canada, and in a few places in the United States, chiefly in Montana. The largest sizes usually encountered are in the 1- to 2-pound range, with lengths of 12 to 16 inches.

True Smelts (Family Osmeridae)

The true, or osmerid, smelts are small inshore fishes of temperate or cold water in the Northern Hemisphere; none of them exceeds 14 inches in length. An important feature in the identification of the true smelt is the presence of a small adipose fin on the dorsal surface of the body, usually opposite the anal fin. This is lacking on the members of the atherinid smelt or silverside family, which is often confused with the osmerid group. About thirteen species of osmerid smelts are known, and most of them are found in the Pacific.

One of the largest members of the family is the eulachon *(Thaleichthys pacificus)*, a 12-inch species of the American Pacific Northwest. It is sometimes called the candlefish because of its oily flesh. The early Indians used the dried

Top: Rainbow trout (Salmo gairdneri); fresh-water.
Bottom: Brook trout (Salvelinus fontinalis); fresh-water.

fish attached to a stick as a torch. In California the delta smelt *(Hypomesus transpacificus)* spends nearly all of its life in the fresh waters of the Sacramento River delta, but this same species in Japan is a marine form, migrating into fresh water only to spawn. The surf smelt *(H. pretiosus)*, is found along the coast from Alaska to southern California. This species lives most of its life in the surf and is an important bait species not only for commercial fishermen but for sport fishermen as well.

Pikes (Family Esocidae)

All members of the Esocid family have ducklike shovel bills and an efficient set of sharp teeth that show when the mouth is agape. These fishes are effective carnivores. Examination of their stomach contents reveals that they are primarily fish eaters, but they also willingly accept frogs, small birds, and mammals. The northern pike *(Esox lucius)* is the most wide-ranging member of the family, found over most of North America from about the latitude of the state of Ohio northward, with the exception of the westernmost portion of the continent. It also occurs throughout many parts of Europe and Asia. In adulthood the northern pike is a large fish with a maximum recorded weight of 46 pounds and a length of 54 inches. The pike follows the family pattern of spawning during the spring months, usually in shallow, weedy areas, where the eggs are scattered indiscriminately.

It is sometimes difficult to identify the various species of pike and other members of the family; however, the scalation along the sides of the head provides the means of differentiation. The northern pike has a complete series of scales from top to bottom on the area of the cheek just behind the eye; on the opercle, which is just posterior to the cheek, only the upper half is scaled. The muskellunge *(E. masquinongy)* has identical scalation on the opercle but can be distinguished from the pike by the fact that only the upper half of the cheek is scaled. If both the cheek and opercle are fully scaled from top to bottom, the fish is one of two pickerels, either the grass pickerel *(E. americanus)*, with dark bands on the sides, or the chain pickerel *(E. niger)*, with chainlike reticulations on the sides.

In size the various species range from an estimated 5 feet 6 inches and 110 pounds for the muskellunge to 24 inches for the chain pickerel and 12 to 14 inches for the grass pickerel. As is well known, the esocids are very important sport and commercial species.

Mudminnows and Blackfish (Family Umbridae)

The mudminnow looks like a junior edition of the pikes and pickerels but has a rounded snout instead of the elongated, shovel-bill profile. The largest of the three species is the central mudminnow *(Umbra limi)*, which may reach a length of 6 inches, although 2 inches or less is the usual size. It is found in silt-bottomed lakes and ponds through the upper Mississippi basin and into the Great Lakes area. The eastern mudminnow *(U. pygmaea)* is a smaller species with a maximum length of about 3 inches; it is found along the Atlantic seaboard from New York to Florida. The third species, the Olympic mudminnow *(Novumbra hubbsi)*, measuring about 4 inches, is known from the Chehalis River in Washington. The name mudminnow is an appropriate one, for these fishes often dig themselves tail first into the mud either to hide or to aestivate. The mudminnows have a remarkable ability to survive in oxygen-deficient water; in fact, they can survive for several days and sometimes weeks in highly viscous mud.

The Alaska blackfish *(Dallia pectoralis)* is an Arctic version of the mudminnow and is as abundant in many of the far northern sections of Arctic America and Siberia as the mudminnows are in the more temperate areas. The blackfish, with its maximum length of 8 inches, is somewhat larger than the mudminnow; it also has a great many more pectoral fin rays: 33 to 36, in contrast to the 18 to 23 of the mudminnow. There are many famous sourdough stories of the ability of the blackfish to withstand cold—how it can actually become frozen in the wintertime and return to its normal activity when the ice thaws. However, it is suspected that its tissues do not actually freeze, for once ice crystals form within the cells of the body, no tissue can regain its normal activity.

Hatchetfishes (Family Sternoptychidae)

All of the approximately 21 species of hatchetfishes are small—less than 3.5 inches in length—and silvery. They have photophores, or light organs, along the lateral margins of the underside of the body, and one genus, *Argyropelecus*, has telescopic eyes aimed upward. These fishes are worldwide in distribution in tropical and temperate waters and are found only in deep waters. In some areas they provide a very important food source for certain species of deep-swimming tuna.

Overleaf: Northern pike (Esox lucius); fresh-water.

Lizardfishes (Family Synodontidae)

Lizardfishes not only look like reptiles but also act like reptiles. Most of their time is spent sitting on the bottom at a slight angle, propped up on the front end by the ventral fins. As soon as small food fishes swim into the area, the lizardfish darts upward with great rapidity, and usually swallows the prey in one gulp.

Most species of lizardfishes are less than 12 inches in length, although there are some, such as the Indo-Pacific *Saurida undosquamis*, that reach a length of 20 inches. Most lizardfishes are inshore shallow-water forms. With the pectoral fins they sometimes burrow down into the sand until only the tips of the eyes show. Some of the lizardfishes are widely distributed; for example, *Synodus synodus* has been able to establish itself on both sides of the tropical Atlantic, and *Trachinocephalus myops* is widely distributed in both the Atlantic and the Pacific. About three dozen species of lizardfishes are recognized; all exhibit the characteristic cylindrical shape and reptile-like head. Most of the species have a small adipose fin on the back between the dorsal and tail fins. Blotched and barred color patterns are typical of the family. The larval form does not even vaguely resemble the adult until it reaches a length of 2 inches or more.

Lancetfishes (Family Alepisauridae)

The lancetfish reaches a length of 6 feet and is equipped with a ferocious set of long, fanglike teeth. On top of the body is a long, high, sail-like dorsal fin that starts just behind the head and extends down the back almost to the small adipose fin just ahead of the tail. There are two species: the shortnose lancetfish *(Alepisaurus brevirostris)* in the Atlantic, and the longnose *(A. ferox)* in both the Atlantic and Pacific. The lancetfishes are the wolves of the mid-water depths of the ocean; they eat everything that gets in their way. Lancetfishes sometimes appear at the surface as a part of the catch of longline fisheries, as a result of sickness or parasite infestation which drives them out of their normal depth, or as a result of ingested food acting like a balloon and forcing them upward.

Barracudinas (Family Paralepididae)

The deep-sea barracudina *(Paralepis atlantica prionosa)* is a pale, usually small, slender-bodied fish with a frightening array of teeth, although a microscope may be required to appreciate this dentition. It is fairly abundant in all mid-ocean depths, except the South Atlantic and the Arctic, down to about 2 miles. The largest barracudina recorded was caught in the Antarctic and measured about 2 feet. Unlike the lanternfishes and others living in the depths, most of the barracudinas are entirely lacking in luminescent light organs. The one known exception is *Lestidium*, which has one or two light-producing organs on the belly. Of the ten genera in the family, the members of only one (*Lestidium*) are known to make vertical migrations. During the day they are found at depths usually greater than half a mile, but at night they move upward almost to the surface. They usually orient themselves vertically, with the head downward.

Lanternfishes (Family Myctophidae)

The lanternfishes, with their neatly arranged photophores along the sides, form a moderately large family of perhaps 150 species. If a light is hung over the side of the ship on a moonless night while the vessel drifts over fairly deep water, and there are lanternfishes about, they will soon be darting around the light. With the approach of day they disappear into the depths, and may be found as much as half a mile down at midday. Lanternfishes are small, the majority in the 3- to 6-inch range, with a few reaching adult size at 1 inch.

Classification of the lanternfishes is dependent on the exact position and number of photophores. For example, two of the main genera are separated by differences in the precaudal photophores. If there are two of these precaudal photophores, the species belongs to the genus *Myctophum*, but if there are three to six, the genus is *Lampanyctus*. One of the common lanternfishes of the Atlantic and Mediterranean, *M. punctatum*, has been studied in detail. It spawns in the Mediterranean during the winter and early spring months.

Spiderfishes (Family Bathypteroidae)

Some characteristics of the spiderfishes of extremely deep seas are strange indeed. The first fin rays of the pelvic fins are greatly elongated and stiffened so that the fish uses them as landing gear, sitting on the bottom with the tips of his pelvic and tail fins forming a resting tripod. The upper fin rays of the pectorals may also be greatly elongated, reaching almost to the tail. About thirteen species are known, most of them in the genus *Bathypterois*.

Milkfishes (Family Chanidae)

Despite its many fine bones, the milkfish *(Chanos chanos)* is usually a valuable food fish throughout its range from the tropical American coast to Africa. It is a large, silvery fish reaching a length of 5 feet. Identification can usually be made through a combination of factors: the dorsal fin opposite the ventrals; the toothless mouth; and the large, deeply forked tail.

The milkfish spawns in shallow, brackish water, usually during the months of March through May. A single fish produces as many as 9,000,000 eggs. In many areas, such as the Philippines, the fry, who measure about half an inch, are collected and transported in special earthenware pots to brackish or fresh-water ponds. There the fry grow rapidly, feeding on the blue-green and green algae which are cultivated as fish food in these ponds. The pond-raised milkfishes are usually harvested during the rainy season, when other marine fishes are scarce in the markets and they can be sold at a maximum price.

CHARACINS, MINNOWS, CATFISHES, AND THEIR RELATIVES (Superorder Ostariophysi)

At least 6,000 kinds of fishes belong to this large group, which is almost entirely confined to fresh water. All of them possess a structure known as the Weberian apparatus, which is actually a series of small bones connecting the air bladder to the internal ear. These bones are formed by modification of the anterior vertebrae and may be a factor in the acuteness of hearing of certain ostariophysan fishes. There is a wide range of variation in external anatomical characteristics, but in general these fishes have their pelvic, or ventral, fins attached near the center of the abdomen, and there is a single dorsal fin with soft rays. Many have an adipose fin.

Ostariophysan fishes are found on all continents with the exception of Australia and Antarctica. Two orders are usually recognized: the Cypriniformes, with three main divisions, the characins, the gymnotid knifefishes, and the minnows, suckers, loaches, and hillstream fishes—a total of at least ten families; and the Siluriformes, with approximately thirty families of catfishes.

Characins or Characids (Family Characidae)

This is the family of the "bloodthirsty" South American piranha and its vege-

Deepsea spiderfish (Bathypterois species); Atlantic-Pacific marine.

tarian cousin so popular with the aquarists—the silver dollar fish. The family was originally known as Characinidae and the fishes as characins. Later the family name was changed to Characidae, with characid becoming the preferred common name. The old name characin is still retained in common usage, however, so that these fishes may be correctly called either name. There is great diversification in body form among this large group of fishes.

The principal distribution of the characins is limited to Central and South America and tropical Africa. These fishes look somewhat like the minnows and carps (family Cyprinidae), but can usually be distinguished from them by the presence of teeth in the jaws; a small, fleshy adipose fin on the back between the dorsal and tail fins; and the absence of the specialized pharyngeal teeth and throat musculature of the minnows. Characins come in many shapes and sizes, the smallest less than 1 inch in length and the largest more than 5 feet long. Some are vegetarians, some are omnivores, and a few are "dangerous" carnivores.

One of the most interesting facts about the fishes of the family Characidae is that anatomically many of them resemble fishes of other groups and families. There are characids that look and act like trout, some that look like North American darters, and one tiny species that looks like a saltwater herring. One species belonging to the genus *Ichthyoelephas*, meaning elephant fish, resembles a sucker (family Catostomidae). A blind characid, *Anoptichthys jordani*, living in caves in Mexico, looks much like the blind African barb, which is of another family.

The breeding habits of most characids are not unusual. The majority of them scatter eggs, which vary in their adhesive qualities, among aquatic plants and tree roots, and then leave the eggs and young to fend for themselves. In many small-sized characids, the male drives the female into a thicket of plants, where she drops her eggs.

In North America there are only about 51 species of characins, and 25 of these do not range farther north than Panama. One of the species with the widest distribution is the 3-inch Mexican tetra *(Astyanax fasciatus)*, which ranges from southern Texas to Argentina and has recently been introduced into California.

There are hordes of small characids with slender to fairly deep bodies, some with beautiful coloring, in Central and South America, and a smaller number in Africa. Many of these small fishes are imported for aquarists. Such names as "glo-lite tetra," "neon tetra," and "head-and-tail-light tetra" speak for themselves. They are truly beautiful fishes with brilliant colors. It may be said that the beautiful and exotic characids are in a large measure responsible for the popularity of the multimillion-dollar tropical fish hobby all over the world.

Gymnotid Eels and Knifefishes (Family Gymnotidae)

This bizarre group of streamlined fishes is anatomically similar to the characids in certain fundamental respects, but much more elongated and without dorsal and ventral fins. Although the gymnotids are obviously related to the characids, there are no known intermediate forms. In spite of the name "eel," which is applied to a number of these fishes, they are not, of course, true eels. An increasingly large number of fishes in this family have been found to have electric organs which enable them to establish electrical fields around their bodies as an aid in the location of enemies, obstacles, and food. The number of discharge impulses per second of these organs may be as high as a thousand, as in the case of the black ghostfish *(Apteronotus albifrons)*.

The gymnotids are usually easy to recognize by such features as the cylindrical to ribbon-like body; small beady eyes; a slender, usually pointed, tail with or without a fin; the absence of a true dorsal fin with fin rays; and, the most important factor, the long, undulating anal fin, which extends along the underside of the body for three fourths to four fifths of the length of the fish. This long fin is responsible for the great mobility of the gymnotids; it enables them to move forward or backward and up or down with equal ease. Some of these fishes have a long, slender, and highly mobile tail that extends beyond the anal fin and is used as a tactile organ, enabling the fish to feel its way backward, where it obviously cannot see.

The gymnotid family as a whole ranges from Nicaragua southward to the River La Plata in Argentina and Paraguay. The total number of species is probably fewer than fifty. The gymnotid eels and knifefishes may be divided into four groups, and some authorities place each of these groups in a separate family.

The best known of all gymnotids is the electric eel *(Electrophorus electricus)*. This 6-foot species and the 4-foot-6-inch *Rhamphichthys rostratus* are both limited to South America and account for two of the four groups. The other two groups are comprised of some seven North American species, four of which do not occur north of Panama. The well-known banded knifefish *(Gymnotus carapo)* ranges as far north as Costa Rica and Nicaragua; it was one of the first knifefishes to be known to the scientific world, having been described by Linnaeus in 1758. The adults may measure 24 inches in length and have about twenty wavy whitish bands around the dark body. Like some other knifefishes, this species is an air breather.

Minnows and Carps (Family Cyprinidae)

The word "minnow" has a variety of meanings, but ichthyologically the term should be restricted to members of the large family Cyprinidae, a predominantly

Blackstripe topminnow (Fundulus notatus); fresh-water.

fresh-water group composed mostly of small fishes. Although the majority of the cyprinids are under 18 inches in length, the range in size is fairly wide, some species being adult at less than 1.5 inches, and others, such as the giant Indian mahseers, reaching lengths of 9 feet. The total number of species in the family probably exceeds 1,500, with more than 300 in the North American fauna, of which 200 are in the United States and Canadian faunas. Minnows occur in all kinds of habitats throughout the temperate and tropical regions of the world with the exception of South America, Madagascar, and Australia. The species range from lethargic, grubbing herbivores to aggressive, predacious carnivores, the majority being omnivorous. With the approach of breeding season, many cyprinid males, and in a few species females, develop conspicuous tubercles on the head or over the entire upper surface of the body.

Minnows have soft rays without true spines; however, in some of the carps and barbs the first ray of the dorsal fin is hardened into a stiff, spinelike structure, and sometimes the first ray of the anal fin is also hardened. They have toothless jaws but compensate for this by having strong throat teeth, which are very important in classification; a number of species are so closely related that the best method of differentiation is by dissection and microscopic examination of the throat teeth. Some species have barbels around the mouth. All minnows lack the adipose fin; the scales are of the cycloid type.

One of the largest American genera of cyprinids is *Notropis*, which has about 100 species, all recognized under common names of various kinds of shiners; examples are the coastal shiner *(N. petersoni)* and the sailfin shiner *(N. hypse-lopterus)*.

One of the most interesting American minnows is the 8-ich stoneroller *(Campostoma anomalum)*, which is widely distributed over the eastern United States; it is noted for the fact that its very long intestine is looped many times around its air bladder. During breeding season the males develop a reddish color and conspicuous tubercles over the upper part of the body. The stoneroller is easily identified by the presence of a narrow black bar on the anal fin and one on the dorsal fin.

Of the several genera of dace, those of the genus *Phoxinus* are among the most brightly colored. The 3-inch southern red-belly dace *(P. erythrogaster)* has along the sides of the body a red stripe bordered by a darker stripe above and below. It ranges from Pennsylvania and Minnesota to Alabama.

A number of species of minnows are found only in western North America. Typical of these fishes are the 12-inch split-tail *(Pogonichthys macrolepidotus)*, which has a deeply forked tail with the upper lobe slightly longer than the lower, and is found in the Sacramento River system of California; and the 3-foot hardhead *(Mylopharodon conocephalus)*, which occurs in the same area.

The chubs of the genus *Hybopsis* include some sixteen or more species of small fishes, the majority less than 4 inches in length. But at least one species, the flathead chub *(H. gracilis)*, occurring throughout most of the central United States, reaches a length of 12 inches.

In some areas the need for live bait for fishing has become critical. To satisfy this need many commercial minnow farms have been established in the south-eastern United States. Some of these may produce as much as 350,000 "head" per acre. Among the most popular production minnows have been the fathead *(Pimephales promelas)*, the goldfish *(Carassius auratus)*, and the golden shiner *(Notemigonus chrysoleucas)*.

The tench, along with some other European species such as the bitterling, rudd, and ide, has been successfully introduced into various American waters. The golden tench *(Tinca tinca)* has two barbels on the mouth and many small scales—usually between 95 and 100—along the lateral line; the number of these scales is often useful in identification. The tench usually occurs in quiet ponds where the bottom is muddy, and it can survive in oxygen-deficient as well as brackish water. Although an 8-pounder is a large fish, specimens have been reported to weigh 17 pounds at a length of some 28 inches.

The strangest reproductive habits among the cyprinids are undoubtedly those of the Central European and now American bitterling *(Rhodeus sericeus)*, a rather deep-bodied species that reaches a length of about 3.5 inches. The female develops a long ovipositor which at breeding season allows the eggs to be passed into the mantle cavity of one of the fresh-water clams or mussels. The eggs incubate and hatch within the living clam. Experimental studies have shown that at least two species of American clams may serve as the host incubator.

The common carp, *Cyprinus carpio*, was originally native to the region from the Black and Caspian seas to Turkestan; from there it has spread by introduction through most of the temperate waters of the world. The carp has four barbels, two at each side of the mouth; these barbels are lacking on the somewhat similar goldfish. Hybrids between carps and goldfishes are common; they usually have very small barbels. The Japanese have developed a golden carp that is a spectacular show fish. Several kinds of aberrant carps are recognized: the most common of these are the mirror carp, in which the abnormally large scales are limited to one or two rows along the sides of the body; and the scaleless leather carp.

The nondescript wild goldfish, *Carassius auratus*, sometimes called johnny carp, Missouri minnow, and in Japan, funa, is a rather plain, brownish, carplike species from which all of the present-day goldfish varieties have been developed, either by natural selection or by artificial breeding. Many different types of domestic goldfishes are recognized, a number of varieties having been pioneered by the Japanese. The comet, with its V-shaped tail, is one of the simpler types; in the United States young fishes of this kind are widely distributed to pet and variety stores and are usually sold for about 25 cents. The veiltail, which has a characteristic three-lobed tail, is another inexpensive, common variety. The blackmoor is a velvety black species with a veil tail and "pop eyes" that extend out from the head. The celestial telescopes usually have the typical goldfish coloration; they do not have a dorsal fin, and the lenses of the bulbous eyes are rotated so that they look upward although the fish is swimming for-

Humpback sucker (Xyrauchen texanus); fresh-water.

ward. The lionheads also lack the dorsal fin and have thick, tumorous-looking material over the forepart of the head. Some of these highly aberrant varieties are difficult to raise, and perfect specimens are sometimes worth several hundred dollars.

The most potentially serious population problem in the cyprinid family is that of the Asiatic grass carp *(Ctenophryngodon idella)*, which has recently been raised by a number of research organizations in the United States. It has been released in open waters in Alabama and perhaps elsewhere. The prodigious growth and high reproductive rate of this herbivore could make it a boon or a curse. If it becomes established, it will most certainly take over the habitats of one or more native species.

Suckers (Family Catostomidae)

The suckers are chiefly an American family and are usually bottom-grubbing fishes. Their fins are arranged in a manner so similar to that of the minnows that identification may at times be difficult, especially since some of the 100 or more described species look like minnows and some of the minnows also look like suckers. Both suckers and minnows have toothless jaws, but generally speaking, the minnow's mouth is at the end of the head, whereas that of the sucker—a highly protrusible, sucking mouth surrounded by large, fleshy lips— is usually located on the underside of the head. One of the principal differences in the two families is in the arrangement of the pharyngeal teeth, which must be removed by dissection in order to be studied. The suckers usually have one row of ten or more fairly fine teeth along the last gill arch, whereas the minnows have fewer teeth in a single row, although sometimes they have two or even three rows, depending upon the species.

The quillback carpsucker *(Carpiodes cyprinus)*, one of four species in the genus, can be identified by its long, flagpole-like second dorsal ray, which is about twice as long as the other rays. It ranges through the central and eastern part of the United States and is a fairly large species, reaching a length of about 26 inches and a weight of about 12 pounds. The redhorse suckers of the genus *Moxostoma* include more than two dozen American species. In all of them the upper lip is very protractile and the lower lip is continuous, with no division in the center. The blacktail redhorse *(M. poecilurum)*, from the coastal streams of the Gulf of Mexico, is one of the most interesting forms; the lower lobe of its tail fin is black and is longer than the upper lobe. One of the most easily

identified suckers is the 18-inch spotted sucker *(Minytrema melanops)*, which has a black spot on each individual scale; it ranges through the larger streams of the eastern United States.

The strangest sucker is the humpback *(Xyrauchen texanus)*, which looks as though it had an inverted boat keel on its back. This keel undoubtedly helps to hold the fish against the bottom in turbulent or fast water. Maximum size is 2 feet and 10 pounds; distribution is limited to the Colorado and Gila rivers' basins.

Loaches (Family Cobitidae)

Since the loach known as the oriental weatherfish *(Misgurnus anguillicaudatus)* has now established populations in Michigan and California, we shall have to consider its family, the Cobitidae, as a part of the American fauna. The loaches are small, usually elongated fishes with six to twelve barbels around the mouth; some of them resemble catfishes, but instead of the typical catfish spines, they have soft-rayed fins, usually with few rays. Some have a movable spine either in front of each eye or below it; the function of this spine is as yet unknown. Although they lack jaw teeth, they usually have pharyngeal teeth. The scales are small and sometimes difficult to see. Because of their method of intestinal respiration, some loaches are able to survive in oxygen-deficient water that would be lethal to other species; they swallow air, and, as it passes through their digestive tracts, they absorb oxygen from it.

The oriental weatherfish is used as food in Japan and other Asiatic areas. I once had lunch at a Tokyo "dojo" restaurant that was 160 years old and served only weatherfish. The fishes were prepared in four different ways, all excellent—if you like weatherfish.

Aquarists have found the loaches to be attractive fishes, so a number of species have been imported for this market. The most interesting loach is probably the European weatherfish *(M. fossilis)*, which is sensitive to changes in barometric pressure. Its increased activity has often been considered a harbinger of stormy weather.

CATFISHES (Order Siluriformes)

The catlike whiskers or barbels extending from the upper jaw and sometimes from the lower jaw provide an easy means of identification of many fishes in

White catfish (Ictalurus catus); fresh-water. 95

this group. Although catfishes do not have scales, a number of them do have bony platelike armor covering the outside of the body. Spines are often present at the front of the dorsal and pectoral fins. These spines may be saw-toothed and may carry venom glands. Certain species have an adipose fin, which may or may not be preceded by a spine, on the back between the dorsal and tail fins.

The Amazon River basin is the center of abundance for the fresh-water cat-fishes, with more than twenty families represented there. Six of these families are also found in Central America, and these include some species of armored catfishes, a group which has long been popular with the aquarist. As one moves northward, the number of families and species decreases until in the United States and Canada only a single fresh-water native catfish family is found, the Ictaluridae.

Most conspicuous of the tropical Central American cats are the long-whiskered members of the family Pimelodidae, especially the species of the large genus *Rhamdia*. One generally thinks of fresh-water fishes as having little if any salinity tolerance, and yet at least two species of catfishes, the long-whiskered *Rhamdia wagneri* and the bullhead *(Ictalurus furcatus)*, are noted for their ability to invade brackish water areas. Similarly, some members of the only American marine catfish family, the Ariidae, are also at home in fresh water.

North American Catfishes (Family Ictaluridae)

In recent years in the southern United States catfish farming has become almost as popular as chinchilla farming was in earlier days, and for the same reason—to augment one's income; catfish are used very heavily in "fish and chips" platters in this region. The catfishes responsible for this boom are all members of the North American catfish family. These ictalurids are "typical" catfishes with four pairs of short barbels around the mouth, an adipose fin, and spines in front of the short dorsal and pectoral fins. The family contains fewer than fifty species, which live in fresh waters from Canada to Guatemala.

One of the most valuable food catfishes is the V-tailed channel cat *(Ictalurus punctatus)*. This species was originally found through most of the central United States but subsequently has been introduced into many other areas. It attains a maximum length of 4 feet and a weight of 57 pounds. The young have spots on the sides, but with growth the channel cat turns dark and the spots are no longer visible.

The bullheads are square-tailed catfishes that provide the fisherman with a low-cost source of protein. The original distribution of the brown bullhead *(I. nebulosus)* was limited to the eastern half of the United States, but like other species of ictalurid catfishes, it has been widely introduced through the western part of North America as well as the Hawaiian Islands and Europe. Brown bullheads are mature at a length of about 6 inches and reach an average maximum length of perhaps 16 inches. These fishes are noted for their care of the young. After the embryos hatch and leave the nest as free-swimming juveniles, they form a dense school which is guarded by one or both of the parents. Other common bullheads include the yellow bullhead *(I. natalis)* and the black bullhead *(I. melas)*, both of which can often be distinguished by their colors.

The white catfish *(I. catus)* was limited in its original distribution to the Atlantic seaboard of the United States. It is slightly larger than the brown bullhead and differs from it in several features, including a pronounced V in its tail.

The smallest members of the North American catfish family are the madtoms, which are also the most dangerous because of the wounds they can inflict with their pectoral spines and associated venom glands. Most of the madtoms are small, with a maximum size of 5 inches. For example, the normal size range of the adult tadpole madtom *(Noturus gyrinus)*, a common form throughout the United States, is from 2 to 3.5 inches. The madtoms can usually be identified by their small size as well as by their very long adipose fin and rounded tail fin; in some madtoms, including the tadpole, these two fins are continuous.

One of the largest ictalurids is the flathead catfish *(Pylodictis olivaris)*, a square-tailed species reported to weigh as much as 100 pounds at a length of about 5 feet 6 inches. The flathead is found throughout the central United States, and it may be identified by the much flattened head and a lower jaw that projects beyond the upper jaw.

The flathead is thought to be the closest relative to the rare widemouth blindcat *(Satan eurystomus)*. This pinkish 2.75-inch species has been captured from the waters of artesian wells more than 1,000 feet deep in the vicinity of San Antonio, Texas. The North American catfish family boasts a second deep-well species from the same Texas area, the toothless blindcat *(Trogloglanis pattersoni)*, which has apparently been derived from *Ictalurus*-type bullheads.

Walking Catfishes (Family Clariidae)

These fresh-water Asiatic catfishes are normally found from Africa to the East

Indies. Throughout their range they are considered valuable food fishes. For this reason, *Clarias fuscus* was introduced to the Hawaiian Islands before 1901; it is now well established, and has never caused any problem. This has not been true of another species, *C. batrachus*, which become popular in the aquarium world only because it had an albino form. In about 1964, a tropical fish dealer north of Fort Lauderdale, Florida, allowed some albino walking cats to escape into nearby canals. These warm waters were quite suitable for the survival of the albino, so that a minor catfish population explosion resulted, with the species spreading to some three counties. The scare publicity that went along with this caused several state fish and game organizations to outlaw not only the albino cat, but all other clariid catfishes as well. It is probable that the Florida catfish population could have been controlled by natural means merely by publishing a recipe for cooking walking catfishes, since, according to some, they are much more tasty than the native American cats. Weather, however, seems to have temporarily solved the problem in Florida with the cold snap of January, 1970, which reduced the walking catfish population to a fraction of its previous number.

Floridians have good reason to be concerned about the introduction of exotic non-native fishes, because they now have some 26 such species established within the state. Fortunately, most of the species are not as tough as the walking catfish, which has an auxiliary breathing apparatus contained in a pocket extending back and upward from the gill cavity. The treelike breathing organ in this special pocket is undoubtedly responsible for the clariid cats' ability to survive out of water much longer than other cats.

Marine Catfishes (Family Ariidae)

The poison-spined plotosid marine catfishes are restricted to Asiatic areas, and only the ariid marine catfishes are found in the Americas. They are found worldwide in the tropics and subtropics, and some are used as food fishes. Unlike many of the fresh-water cats, they do not spend their time resting on the bottom, but are always on the move, often in a school formation. They have four to six barbels around the mouth and the usual complement of predorsal and pectoral spines; they also have an adipose fin. However, they differ from other catfishes in that the anterior and posterior nostrils are closer together, the latter covered by a valve. In the North American fauna there are about seventeen species of ariid catfishes found north of Panama. Although some

Top: Albino walking catfish (Clarias batrachus); fresh-water.
Bottom: Sea catfish (Arius felis); Atlantic marine and fresh-water.

enter rivers and lakes, there are two species belonging to the genus *Potamarius* that are restricted to the fresh waters of Guatemala and southeastern Mexico.

Some forty species of ariid catfishes are known to be mouthbreeders, with the male usually incubating the eggs. Normally, the brooding of the eggs takes place in saltwater, but it can also occur in fresh water, depending on the species. On the Atlantic coast the common sea catfish *(Arius felis)*, up to 2 feet in size, ranges from Cape Cod to Panama. The male carries up to 55 eggs in his mouth for almost a month before hatching takes place. For the next two months he continues to hold the youngsters in his mouth and does not take food during this time.

The gafftopsail catfish *(Bagre marinus)*, also up to 2 feet in size, is another Atlantic species ranging from Cape Cod through the Gulf of Mexico and the West Indies. It can be instantly identified by the extended rays of the dorsal fin. Underwater audio specialist William Tavolga has found that this species produces at least three kinds of sounds, which may be used under variable circumstances: in holding the school together, in establishing dominance by a single individual, or as the result of extreme stress.

On the Pacific coast there are fewer species of seacats, the most common being the chihuil *(B. panamensis)*; it ranges from southern California to Panama.

The cleaned skull of an ariid catfish viewed from the underside often has the appearance of a cross, sometimes with the figure of a man superimposed. In the West Indies and along the coasts of South America these skulls are often sold to gullible tourists as native religious objects of sacred value.

Long-whiskered Catfishes (Family Pimelodidae)

The pimelodids are the largest family of South American catfishes. Their distribution extends northward as far as Mexico. About 23 species occur in the area between Panama and the Veracruz region of Mexico, and most of these are members of the genus *Rhamdia*. Characteristically, these fishes have three pairs of very long whiskers or barbels plus an adipose fin and spines in front of the dorsal and pectoral fins.

CAVEFISHES, TROUTPERCHES, AND PIRATEPERCH (Order Percopsiformes)

These three families are the only living representatives of a formerly widespread transitional group of North American fishes with characteristics intermediate between the more primitive troutlike forms and the more advanced spiny-rayed fishes.

Cavefishes (Family Amblyopsidae)

The North American amblyopsid family is a favorite with cave investigators because its six species live everywhere from exposed surfaces of the earth to the deepest caves. The maximum length of these whitish fishes is about 3.5 inches. Four species have distributions closely correlated with the limestone formations of the eastern United States, having been found in the Mississippi basin between 39 and 32 degrees latitude. The exception is the surface-living swampfish *(Chologaster cornuta)*, which seems to have no correlation with limestone areas and lives entirely apart from the other four species; it is found on the Atlantic coastal plain from Virginia to central Georgia. It does not occur in caves but is found in streams and cypress swamps where the temperatures may range between 39° and 80° F.

The other species in the family include the spring cavefish *(C. agassizi)*, the Ozark cavefish *(Amblyopsis rosae)*, the northern cavefish *(A. spelaea)*, the southern cavefish *(Typhlichthys subterraneus)*, and a relict undescribed species from a cave in northwestern Alabama.

One feature that all the amblyopsids have in common is sensory papillae, or tactile organs, in quite prominent rows on the head, body, and tail; the arrangement of these rows of papillae varies with different species. There are also additional tactile organs beneath the epidermis. These sensory organs help make up for the lack of vision in the blind fishes and the rudimentary vision in the eyed forms.

The two species of *Amblyopsis* are distinguished from the other members of the family by the presence of two or three rows of sensory papillae on each half of the tail fin. In addition, the northern cavefish *(A. spelaea)* has small pelvic fins, which are not present in any of the other members of the family.

The swampfish mentioned above *(Chologaster cornuta)*, with its non-cave habitat, obviously has need of functional eyes, which it has. This is also true to a lesser extent of its cousin, the spring cavefish *(C. agassizi)*. These two species can be distinguished by the number of rays in the tail fin (nine to eleven in *C. cornuta* and twelve to sixteen in *C. agassizi*) and by a dark streak present on the sides of the former but absent on the latter. Laboratory experiments with

Chologaster have shown that individuals with their functional eyes removed can find their food and survive as well as they did with their eyes.

The other three described species of amblyopsids are blind, although they retain a rudimentary eye. Normally these fishes lack pigment; however, it has been noted that the southern cavefish *(Typlichthys subterraneus)*, when kept in daylight in an aquarium for three months, gradually developed a dusky color, the pigment being compacted into a wide mid-lateral band with a series of oblique marks at the division points of the muscle segments.

There has been much speculation about the distribution of these fishes. Some of the species are rather widely distributed in places where migration by surface water would seem highly unlikely for these blind fishes. For example, *Typhlichthys* is found on each side of the Ozark plateau, a distance of only 75 miles by land but over 1,000 miles by surface water. The area in which *Typhlichthys* and *Amblyopsis* are found is known to be underlined with subterranean limestone channels of water that flow beneath the rivers and surface streams, and it is believed that these channels are used as a means of dispersal by these fishes. One species, the spring cavefish *(Chologaster agassizi)*, is known to migrate for short distances by surface waters, but is thought to utilize the underground passages as well.

The actual breeding of these fishes has not been observed, but it is known that the *Amblyopsis* female carries the eggs in the gill chamber. In laboratory specimens caught in the wild, these eggs, about seventy in number, hatched after about two months into young measuring three-eights of an inch. It is believed that this method of breeding may be characteristic of all of the amblyopsid family.

Troutperches (Family Percopsidae)

The blunt-nosed troutperch *(Percopsis omiscomaycus)*, sometimes called the sandroller, is a 6-inch spotted fish that can be identified by its adipose fin, spiny fins, and rough spiny scales. It is found in most of Canada, ranging from Quebec to the eastern border of British Columbia and southward to Kansas, Missouri, Kentucky, and Virginia. In the Great Lakes it is a forage fish of some importance and is found abundantly in shallow areas; however, it also occurs in depths up to 200 feet. Spawning takes place in the spring in shallow areas.

The second species of troutperches *(Columbia transmontana)* occurs in the Columbia River basin of western North America. Like *Percopsis*, it has the

Blind cave characin (Anoptichthys jordani); fresh-water.

identifying adipose fin as well as two spines in front of both the dorsal and the anal fins; but unlike *Percopsis*, it has only one spine preceding the anal fin rather than two. It is a smaller species, being full grown at 3 to 4 inches.

Pirateperch (Family Aphredoderidae)

The 5-inch adult pirateperch *(Aphredoderus sayanus)* has a surprising anatomical peculiarity that distinguishes it from other fishes. As the fish grows, the vent, which in the juvenile is in the normal position just ahead to the anal fin, moves forward until in the adult fish it is located underneath the throat, just behind the gill openings. The pirateperch usually has one pelvic, two anal, and three dorsal fin spines, but it lacks the adipose fin. It occurs along the Atlantic coast from New York to Texas, then northward through the Mississippi basin as far as Michigan. Its preferred habitat is ponds and lakes where there is much debris and organic decomposition on the bottom.

Oyster toadfish (Opsanus tau); Atlantic marine.

TOADFISHES AND MIDSHIPMEN
(Order Batrachoidiformes)

Toadfishes are slow-moving, bottom-dwelling fishes with large mouths equipped with many sharp teeth. The heavy, broad head is depressed anteriorly and tapers to a long, slender tail. The small first dorsal fin with two to four spines is followed by a long, soft-rayed dorsal fin. In all members of the family the spines of the first dorsal fin are solid except in the genera *Thalassophryne* and *Thalassothia*. The pelvic fins are placed under the throat ahead of the fanlike pectoral fins. Only three pairs of gills are present. The toadfishes are found from shallow to deep water in temperate and tropical seas, and a few occur in brackish and fresh water. About forty species are known.

The bagre sapo toadfishes *(Thalassophryne* and *Thalassothia)* of the tropical American coasts possess an extremely efficient venom-injection apparatus similar to the fangs of rattlesnakes. They have two large dorsal fin spines and a spine at the edge of each gill cover; each of these spines is hollow and has a poison gland at its base.

A number of these fishes make migrations from deep to very shallow water and later return; these migrations are often correlated with spawning activities. They are able to live out of water, sometimes for several hours, and can survive in oxygen-deficient water that would be lethal to most other fishes. Most toadfishes and midshipmen make some sort of sound, usually grunts or raucous growls or a single boat-whistle blast. The sound is usually produced by the air bladder. The oyster toadfish *(Opsanus tau)* is a shallow-water 10-inch fish common along many sections of the coast from Maine to Florida; there are similar species in the Gulf of Mexico.

The midshipmen of the genus *Porichthys* are noted for numerous photophores arranged in linear patterns on the head and body. In laboratory experiments these can be made to light up.

CLINGFISHES *(Order Gobiesociformes)*

A large adhesive sucker under the forward part of the body enables the clingfish to maintain an attachment to rocks and seaweed in shallow water, usually in the intertidal zone. The anterior part of the sucker is formed from the pelvic fins; the posterior part is a fold of skin. Clingfishes have a single dorsal fin without spines. All of the approximately 100 species are small and have very broad heads that taper off to slender bodies. They are chiefly a tropical and temperate marine group with a few species occurring in the fresh-water streams of Panama and the Galapagos Islands. One of the larger species is the 6-inch northern clingfish *(Gobiesox maeandricus)*, which ranges from California to Alaska. In the Atlantic one of the most delicate and beautiful species is the 1-inch emerald clingfish *(Acyrtops beryllina)*, which ranges from Florida and the Bahamas through the Antilles and the western Caribbean.

Overleaf, left: Gulf toadfish (Opsanus beta); Atlantic marine.
Right: Sargassumfish (Histrio histrio); Atlantic marine.

ANGLERFISHES (Order Lophiiformes)

One of the distinctions of many of the anglerfishes, a group of some sixteen families that are chiefly deep-sea forms, is a lure at the end of a movable whip-like rod that resembles a fishing pole and is suspended over the mouth. The whole fishing pole is a modified first spiny ray of the dorsal fin. The angler moves the lure back and forth as though it is fly fishing. These fishes move very slowly, but when live food is nearby, they can gulp or siphon it into the mouth with such speed that the human eye cannot follow its movement. More than 225 species of anglerfishes are known.

The deep-sea anglers include some eleven families and about 120 species, all of which differ from the other anglers by the absence of the ventral fins. Whereas many of the anglers live on the bottom from shallow to deep water, or, in a few cases, at the surface, the deep-sea anglers are mostly mid-water forms, ranging in depths from perhaps one thousand to several thousand feet. Among the deep-sea species only the females have fishing poles. Since in the depths it would be difficult for the potential prey to see the lure, the tip is usually equipped with a light-producing organ of some kind.

Four families of the deep-sea anglers demonstrate a most surprising biological phenomenon: the males are parasitic on the females. The males never grow very large, and at an early age they attach themselves by their mouths to the much larger females and become permanently anchored, their circulation fusing with that of the female. Thus the male becomes nothing but a sperm-producing appendage.

Goosefishes (Family Lophiidae)

These repulsive-looking fishes are among the largest of the anglers. Some reach a length of 4 feet and a weight of 45 pounds, and there is a record of one that weighed 70 pounds. In spite of their ugly appearance, their meat is excellent, and they are marketed as food in northern Europe and Japan though not in the Americas. The goosefish spends its time on the bottom, often camouflaged against its background. It is an odd-shaped fish: the width of the huge, flattened head is about two thirds of the length of the fish. The mouth is almost as wide as the head and is armed with a battery of wicked-looking teeth. A fringe of small flaps extends around the lower jaw and along the sides of the head onto the body. The fishing pole, modified from the first of six dorsal fin spines, has at its tip a flap of flesh that acts like a flag as the goosefish whips it back and forth in front of its mouth.

The goosefish is apparently very successful at stalking its prey, for the food in the crammed stomach may weigh as much as one third of the total weight of the fish. Anything that moves is fair prey, including sea birds, small sharks, all kinds of fishes, and crabs.

Spawning takes place during the spring and summer. The eggs, which float at the surface, are embedded in a sticky, jelly-like mass that may measure forty feet in length and two feet in width. The strange-looking larval fishes have extremely long ventral fins, which gradually diminish in size as the fish grows to maturity.

Goosefishes and monkfishes are found in tropical and temperate marine waters of the world except in the eastern Pacific. About a dozen species are recognized. On the American Atlantic coast *Lophius americanus* occurs from Newfoundland to Brazil; it is found in shallow water in the north and in deep water near the equator.

Frogfishes (Family Antennariidae)

In some frogfishes, such as the Atlantic American splitlure frogfish *(Antennarius scaber)* and the sargassumfish *(Histrio histrio)*, the fishing pole and its conspicuous lure are well developed and used to great advantage to attract prey. But in other species, including a number in the Indo-Pacific, the fishing pole is slender, wirelike, and without a lure. When live food is in the vicinity, these fish wave the pole back and forth in the same manner as do others in the family, but with them it seems to be totally ineffective. Food capture is dependent upon the speed of the frogfish and not upon the lure. The carnivorous frogfishes have balloon-shaped bodies covered with loose skin that is usually roughened by many small denticles. The females extrude their eggs in the form of a long, ribbon-like mass that floats at the surface.

Frogfishes are found around the world in all tropical and temperate seas. Some 65 species are recognized, of which nine are in the western Atlantic and only a very few in the eastern Pacific. Most species are bottom dwellers, often hidden in coral or rocks. The amazing sargassumfish reverses the family pattern and is pelagic among sargassum weed. The pectoral fins of this fish are remarkable because of their prehensile ability; they actually clasp the weed as the angler moves slowly through the drifting sargassum.

Batfishes (Family Ogcocephalidae)

Like an armored tank, the comical batfish waddles across the bottom on its large armlike pectoral and small leglike ventral fins. It occasionally gets up off the bottom and swims awkwardly as if entirely unaccustomed to this method of progression. The bat's fishing pole is hidden in a small tube just above the mouth. Whenever the batfish is angling for food, the pole is pushed out of the tube and is usually rotated so that the hinged, lumplike lure at the tip is vibrated to either the right or the left, depending upon the individual fish. In an aquarium some batfishes always vibrate the lure to the left. The sixty or so species of batfishes are the most modified of all the anglers; they are flat-bodied, scaleless marine forms living in tropical and temperate waters. There are fourteen species in the western Atlantic and fewer in the eastern Pacific. The largest are about 15 inches in length, but most of them are less than half that size. Although the family is primarily a deep-water group, there are a number of shallow-water species.

The 15-inch shortnose batfish *(Ogcocephalus nasutus)* is one of the common Caribbean species. The smaller pancake batfish *(Halieutichthys aculeatus)* has a distinctive pancake-shaped body; it ranges from the Carolinas through the Gulf of Mexico and the lesser Antilles.

CODFISHES, HAKES, RATTAILS, AND BROTULAS (Order Gadiformes)

The codfishes and their relatives have soft-rayed fins, usually without spines. They may often be identified by the "cod look," which is partially characterized by the location of the pelvic fins ahead of the pectorals, sometimes under the throat. Another typical feature is the presence of a ductless air bladder. Certain of the deep-sea grenadiers or rattails have a single spine in front of the dorsal fin. A few of the cods and a larger number of grenadiers have luminous glands or ducts that produce light by means of luminescent bacteria. As many as eleven families of gadiform fishes are sometimes recognized, with a total of several hundred species.

Codfishes (Family Gadidae)

The gadids are predominantly a cold- and temperate-water group and with

Top: Shortnose batfish (Ogcocephalus nasutus); Atlantic marine.
Bottom: Pacific cod (Gadus macrocephalus); Pacific marine.

one exception are all marine fishes; they occur chiefly in the Northern Hemisphere and to a lesser extent in the Southern Hemisphere. The family includes some of the world's most valuable food fishes. Since many of these forms live near the bottom, they are often called ground or bottom fishes. Because of the capacity of dried and salted codfish to remain edible, fisheries for the Atlantic cod *(Gadus morhua)* are among the world's oldest; it has long been one of the most profitable food fishes on both sides of the North Atlantic. The Atlantic cod has a characteristic speckled pattern on the sides of the body, three dorsal fins, two anal fins, and a small, whiskery barbel under the chin. It is the largest of some 150 species in the family, reaching a maximum of 211 pounds at a length of 6 feet; those caught commercially, however, are usually much smaller, ranging from only 2.5 to 25 pounds. Spawning generally takes place between January and March, with the female laying a great number of eggs, the record being about 9,000,000 for a 75-pound fish. The eggs float for some ten to twenty days, and as soon as they hatch, the larval cods become part of the floating plankton, in which state they remain for the next two and a half months. By this time they have reached a length of about 1 inch; they then sink to the bottom where they continue to grow fairly rapidly. In two years the cods reach a length of about 15 inches; by the time they are five years old, they are usually capable of spawning.

The smoked fish product called finnan haddie is widely known to many who may not be familiar with the actual fish, *Melanogrammus aeglefinus*, the haddock. This species resembles the cod in having three dorsal and two anal fins, but it lacks the cod's reticulated markings along the sides of the body. A large blotch just above and behind the pectoral fin provides ready identification. It is a much smaller fish than the cod, the maximum recorded size being 44 inches and 36 pounds. It is widely distributed on both sides of the North Atlantic, and recently has been the basis for highly productive bottom fisheries in both regions.

Another commercially important North Atlantic species is the pollock *(Pollachius virens)*, a fish with greenish coloration on the upper part of the body and a jutting lower jaw usually without a barbel under the chin.

The Pacific tomcod *(Microgadus proximus)* is a 12-inch silvery white species ranging from Alaska to central California; although it is highly esteemed by some as a food item, the total sports and commercial catch is small. The Atlantic tomcod *(Microgadus tomcod)* is slightly larger than the Pacific species, and occasionally moves into fresh water throughout its range from the Gulf of St. Lawrence to Virginia.

Spotted cusk-eel (Otophidium taylori); Pacific marine.

The Pacific cod *(Gadus macrocephalus)* has a mottled pattern along the sides of the body somewhat like the Atlantic cod, but it is a smaller species, its maximum length being only about 39 inches. It ranges from California to the Bering Sea and south to Japan and Korea. On the American side it is of negligible commercial importance, but in Japan it is one of the most valuable food fishes.

Because the hakes have the frontal bones of the head separate (those of the cod are joined) and ribs attached to the anterior vertebrae (in the cod the ribs begin with the fifth or sixth vertebra), some investigators consider them members of a separate family, the Merlucciidae. Externally, the elongated, streamlined hakes look like many of the other codfishes. In the hake the second and third dorsals are combined to form a single, very long second dorsal fin, which has a slight notch in the center. A center notch is also present on the very long single anal fin. The pelvic fins are located ahead of the pectoral fins, the lower jaw is longer than the upper jaw, and there are no barbels under the chin. The flesh of the hakes is fairly soft and usually does not keep as well as that of most other fishes. The silver hake *(Merluccius bilinearis)* is the common Atlantic American species, and its relative on the West Coast is the Pacific hake *(M. productus)*.

The only fresh-water member of the cod family—and of the entire order—is the burbot *(Lota lota)*, a Holarctic species which ranges from the polar regions southward in Eurasia and North America. Since it is the only fresh-water fish that has codfish characteristics, it is fairly easy to identify. The burbot is a very slender fish, the largest on record measuring 32 inches and weighing only 12 pounds. It is a winter spawner, with the young appearing during the early spring. The eggs, instead of floating, as those of the marine species do, lie on the bottom. It is a cold-water as well as a deep-water species, having been taken at depths of 700 feet in the Great Lakes.

Cusk-eels and Brotulas (Family Ophidiidae)

Members of the Ophidiid family have very slender pelvic fins which may be attached either under the chin, as in the cusk-eels, or further back under the gill area, as in the brotulas. Among the cusk-eels, and to a lesser extent the brotulas, whisker-like chin and throat fins are used as sensors, with the extended fins being dragged across the bottom. Both dorsal and anal fins have a great many rays beginning just behind the head and extending to the tail, which is usually pointed. Although some forty species of cusk-eels and perhaps 170 species

114   *Red brotula (Brosmophycis marginata); Pacific marine.*

of brotulas are recognized, the list of common names shows only fifteen cusk-eels and seven brotulas in United States and Canadian waters. Actually, the family is more tropical marine than temperate marine in distribution. Although most cusk-eels are less than 12 inches long when full grown, there are others that grow to a much larger size. The rare 4-foot deep-sea *Parabassogigas grandis* has been captured off the Oregon and California coasts. In South Africa the famed deep-water kingklip *(Genypterus capensis)*, found in water 180 to 1,500 feet deep, reaches a length of 5 feet and is considered a great delicacy. The spotted cusk-eel *(Otophidium taylori)*, captured along the California coast, proved to be a tail-stander when kept in an aquarium tank for the first time; this was a previously unknown characteristic.

The brotulids are a highly variable group, not only anatomically but also in habitat. They range from the greatest depths of the ocean to fresh-water caves; both habitats have some blind species. The only fish ever taken at a depth of more than 4 miles belonged to the brotulid genus *Bassogigas;* it was a small, 6.25-inch specimen dredged in the Sunda trench by the Galathea Expedition in 1951.

The red brotula *(Brosmophycis marginata)* ranges from Alaska to southern California in water of moderate depths. Like many other members of the family it is secretive and seldom observed. An individual captured during a night dive in Monterey Bay has lived for seven years in its own 26-gallon tank at Steinhart Aquarium in San Francisco.

Cucumber and Pearl Fishes (Family Carapidae)

As adults these slender, knifelike "fierasfers," as they are sometimes called, are usually tail borers, hiding within cracks and crevices by entering them tail first. Often these hiding places are living animals such as sea cucumbers (holothurians), clams, starfishes, sea urchins, and even tunicates. The name "pearl fish" is derived from the fact that the host for some species is the pearl shell; on at least one occasion the fish has been permanently trapped by the shell and become embedded in it like an abnormal pearl.

The life history of a typical cucumber fish is very interesting. Although actual egg laying has not been recorded, the eggs are known to float at the surface, soon hatching into larvae that pass through two different stages before beginning to look like the adult. Either as a second-stage larva or as a subsequent juvenile, the cucumber fish proceeds to find an appropriate host. Stomach contents of

116

some cucumber fishes indicate that they feed on the reproductive organs and branchial gills within the host.

About thirty species are recognized. All share the anatomical peculiarity of having the vent far forward under the throat. They lack scales and pelvic and tail fins, and one group of three species of *Encheliophis* has even lost the pectoral fins. The dorsal and anal fins begin a short distance behind the head and are continuous to the tip of the pointed tail.

The largest members of this family (*Echiodon drummondi* from the British Isles and Scandinavian waters and *Carapus parvipinnis* from the Pacific) reach a length of 12 inches. Most of the remaining species are less than 6 inches in length, although the single western Atlantic pearl fish *(Carapus bermudensis)* is slightly larger, reaching 7 inches. The cucumber and pearl fishes are normally considered shallow-water species; however, some of them have been taken in water as deep as 600 feet. The family has a worldwide distribution in tropical and subtropical waters, although one or two hardier species are found in temperate seas.

Eelpouts (Family Zoarcidae)

In the marine zoarcid eelpouts the dorsal and anal fins extend around the tail, which comes to a point; the pelvic fins are minute and are located just back of the gills but ahead of the pectorals. The upper jaw projects over the lower jaw, and the lips are quite thick. About 55 species are known, most of them less than 18 inches in length. They live in cold sea water that ranges from very shallow to depths of more than a mile. Many give birth to living young. However, the 3-foot American Atlantic ocean pout *(Macrozoarces americanus)* lays eggs; these are one fourth of an inch in diameter and are guarded by one or both parents. The zoarcids are common fishes in the waters of both the Arctic and the Antarctic.

Deepsea Rattails and Grenadiers (Family Macrouridae)

Rattails are so named because of their long, tapering tails. The tail fin is usually missing, and the long anal and second dorsal fins extend almost to the pointed tip of the body. As in the codfishes, the pelvic fins are anterior to the pectorals in position. Some species have a single spine in front of the flaglike first dorsal fin; many have a barbel under the chin. Although there are many genera and species of grenadiers living in the depths of all the oceans, some in tremendous abundance, they are seldom seen, since only occasionally do they stray into water even as shallow as 500 feet. In the American fauna, only the Atlantic marlin-spike *(Nezumia bairdi)* enters shore waters. The majority of the species are less than 2 feet in length, although some grow much larger.

FLYINGFISHES, TOPMINNOWS AND SILVERSIDES (Order Atheriniformes)

This important order contains some 16 families of which we shall consider eight. There are three distinct subgroups within the order: (a) needlefishes, flyingfishes including halfbeaks, and sauries; (b) egg-laying topminnows (killifishes), live-bearing topminnows, four-eyed fishes and goodeids, and (c) silversides.

Needlefishes (Family Belonidae)

Examination of the mouth of a needlefish leads to the conclusion that it is well named, for these long-jawed, ferocious fishes are armed with many fine teeth, which are capable of wreaking havoc among schools of smaller fishes as well as on unwary fishermen. In appearance, the needlefishes are similar to the fresh-water gars of North America or the marine barracudas, but they are probably faster than either. They are tremendous jumpers, and at times it seems almost as though they are trying to become flyingfishes. Most of the approximately 26 species are found in all tropical and temperate marine waters and are usually confined to saltwater; some species do move into fresh water, however, and a very few live permanently in fresh water. Several species, including the Indo-Pacific *Strongylura crocodilus* and the Atlantic *S. marina*, reach lengths of 3 feet 6 inches to 4 feet; the majority of species, however, are mature at less than 2 feet.

Flyingfishes and Halfbeaks (Family Exocoetidae)

Does a flyingfish actually fly? This question has been debated down through the ages, and only in recent years have high-speed photographic studies enabled us to learn that the adult flyingfish normally does not vibrate its wings during flight, but holds them relatively steady. The powerful tail drives the fish up out

Pearl fish (Carapus bermudensis) and host (sea cucumber); Atlantic marine.

of the water and the extended wings provide a glider-type flight. To have true birdlike flight, the wings would need to vibrate sufficiently to support the body in the air; only among the South American fresh-water hatchetfishes and, to a lesser extent, the African fresh-water butterflyfishes is such ability found. For the flyingfish, the average flight speed is about 35 miles an hour, and flights as long as thirteen seconds have been clocked. Although most flights are close to the water, at night some fishes have been known to fly aboard ships whose decks were 20 feet above the water.

Many of the juveniles are quite different from the adults, not only because of their variegated color pattern but also because of a pair of large flaplike whiskers that extend downward from the tip of the lower jaw. In some species these whiskers may be longer than the fish itself; for example, a 2-inch juvenile of the Caribbean *Cypselurus cyanopterus* has whisker streamers extending beyond the tail. With growth, these appendages are lost, which explains why juvenile flyingfishes have in the past been described as a species different from their parents.

Identification of a flyingfish is not difficult because of the enlarged "flying fins" and, of course, the lopsided tail, with its lower lobe much longer than the upper. The fins are without spines. Flyingfishes are generally found offshore, usually over deep water; however, there are some inshore forms occurring only in coastal waters. At present about fifty species of flyingfishes are recognized. Watching flyingfishes as they scatter in front of a ship, one is able to divide them into two categories—the two-wing and the four-wing types. The two-wing flyingfish has two very large pectoral fins and small, inconspicuous pelvics, while the four-wing type has pelvic fins nearly as large as the pectorals. The four-wing types are noted for the beautiful color patterns on their wings.

Deepsea rattail (at 4,000 feet depth); Pacific marine.

California flyingfish (Cypselurus californicus); Pacific marine.

The largest of the flyingfishes is a four-wing species, *Cypselurus californicus*, an 18-inch form that has a limited distribution along the coasts of southern California and Baja California. It is caught commercially during the late spring and summer months; some of the catch is sold in the fresh-fish market, and the remainder is used as bait for swordfish and tuna. The Atlantic *C. heterurus* is the most common four-wing flyingfish found on both sides of the Atlantic; on the American side its range is from the Gulf of Maine to Rio de Janeiro. It has an oblique band extending across the forward wings, and at maximum size it is about 12 inches in length. Important two-wing species include the 10-inch *Exocoetus volitans*, which occurs around the world in tropical waters; it has a smooth, buoyant egg without the long tendrils characteristic of most flyingfish eggs.

121

If the long upper jaw were removed from a longsnouted needlefish but the lower jaw were left intact and the size decreased to no more than 12 or at most 18 inches, the result would look like a halfbeak. This peculiar group includes about sixty species, many of which are marine, whereas others are restricted to fresh water. The halfbeaks have short pectoral fins, which does not prevent their trying to act like flyingfishes; some of them make short, skittering flights. A further indication of their close relationship to the flyingfishes is shown by the flyingfish type of lopsided tail possessed by some species.

Most halfbeaks fertilize their eggs externally, as do the majority of other fishes, but a few have internal fertilization and young that are born alive. *Hyporhamphus unifasciatus* is one of the most widely distributed of the halfbeaks. It is found in the eastern Pacific and on both sides of the Atlantic; on American shores it occurs from Maine to Argentina.

Sauries (Family Scomberesocidae)

From the standpoint of abundance, the sauries are very important members of the offshore fauna of the world's tropical and temperate seas. They resemble the needlefishes but have short jaws, and they may be identified by a series of two sets of five to seven finlets, one series after the dorsal and the other after the anal fin. Four species are recognized; all of them are small, 12 to 14 inches being the maximum size. In Japan there are important fisheries for *Cololabis saira*, a species that is also common off the American Pacific coast. *Scomberesox saurus* is a common Mediterranean species that ranges up the European coast and across the Atlantic to the United States.

Egg-laying Topminnows: Killifishes (Family Cyprinodontidae)

The threat of extinction has brought members of this family, known as the Death Valley pupfishes, into national prominence. Whereas in past years enthusiastic aquarists often made collecting trips to Death Valley and adjacent areas containing isolated desert springs, such collecting is now banned by state and federal regulations. Thirteen forms of pupfishes (including eight *Cyprinodon* and four *Empetrichthys*) have been recognized from this region, and, largely because of man's carelessness, five of these are already extinct. Pupfishes have been and are being eliminated by the introduction of non-native fishes, alteration of habitat, underground pumping, and accidental pesticide poisoning.

Pike killifish (Belonesox belizanus); fresh-water.

The 2.5-inch pupfish is extremely adaptable. It is able to swim actively in water less than an inch deep, it can survive in mud puddles, and it can flip its body between small pools of water. It has the ability to live in water with greatly fluctuating temperatures, and can live in water as hot as 112° F. It tolerates saline concentrations six times greater than normal sea water. Some also have the ability to hibernate in mud through the cold winters.

The pupfishes and their relatives, in addition to being recognized as cyprinodont topminnows, are sometimes called egg-laying tooth carps. The family includes more than 300 species, many of which have been popularized by aquarists. The largest species are about 6 inches when full grown, but the majority are much smaller. Nothing compares with the thrill of capturing fishes for one's own home aquarium, which is another reason for the popularity of this group. Locally available fishes in the East include species such as the beautiful golden topminnow *(Fundulus chrysotus)*, which ranges from South Carolina to Florida in fresh and brackish water, and the attractive starhead topminnow *(F. notti)*, which has banded males and striped females and ranges through the central and southeastern United States.

123

The California killifish *(F. parvipinnis)* is a tidepool species which is probably the least spectacular in the genus, but like its relatives it adapts readily to aquarium life. Its counterpart in the eastern United States is the mummichog *(F. heteroclitus)*.

Florida has some outstanding members in this family, such as the spectacular 2-inch flagfish *(Jordanella floridae)* and the pygmy killifish *(Leptolucania ommata)*, which is noted for the large ocellus on the side of the caudal peduncle just in front of the tail fin. A pre-tail spot is also found on rivulus *(Rivulus marmoratus)*, a species living in southern Florida, Cuba, and the Bahamas. Some hermaphroditic rivulus can function as male and female at the same time. Externally, these self-fertilizing fish look like females, but they will not pair with other fish of the same species.

The 1.5-inch rainwater killifish *(Lucania parva)*, the smallest species in the family, has on several occasions been accidentally introduced from the southeastern and southern United States into the western states. Established populations now exist in Utah, Oregon, and central and southern California.

The small group of topminnows known as annuals are noted for their short life cycles, which are usually less than one year. Each species is carried over during the dry season in the egg stage. Although primarily African and South American in distribution, there are also some North American species that are suspected of having the capacity to become annuals. For example, recent investigations have shown that the unhatched eggs of the common marsh killifish *(Fundulus confluentus)* may remain alive and hatchable after as much as a three-month exposure. When the eggs are immersed in tap water, hatching occurs in fifteen to thirty minutes.

Livebearing Topminnows (Family Poeciliidae)

The Reverend Robert John Lechmere Guppy little suspected when he discovered some small, beautiful fishes with long streamer-like tails on the island of Trinidad in 1866 that his name would be made known to millions by this little 2.5-inch fish, *Poecilia reticulata*, commonly called the guppy. Like other members of this family, guppy young are born alive. They reproduce so rapidly that at one time they were called millions fishes. Internal fertilization is normal for the family; the males have spermatophores, or masses of sperm, which are transferred during copulation to the oviduct and remain there to fertilize several successive batches of eggs. The male copulatory organ or gonopodium is formed from the

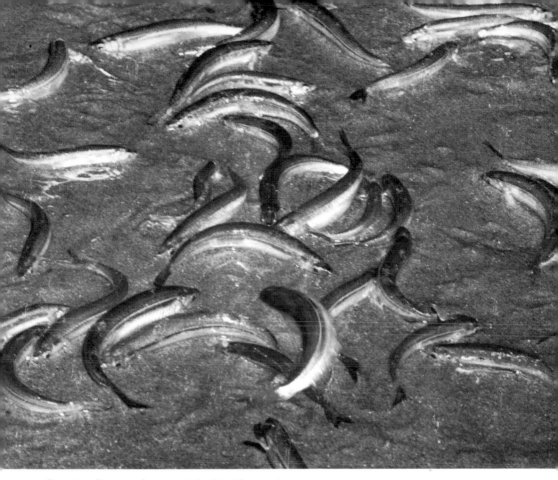

Grunion (Leuresthes tenuis); Pacific marine.

elongated anterior rays of the anal fin. The gonopodial rays are much longer than the other anal fin rays, a feature that instantly identifies the males of any species in the family. The anal fin of the female is usually rounded and lacks the extended rays. Full-grown female guppies measure about 2 inches in length, whereas the males are usually about half as long. Their normal habitat extends from the islands of the southern Caribbean to the southern part of Brazil.

The family Poeciliidae is a large one, with more than 45 genera and a great number of species. They are entirely New World fishes, ranging from Illinois and New Jersey in the United States to Argentina.

One of the peculiarities found in the poeciliid family is that some species produce only female offspring. Dr. and Mrs. Carl Hubbs made the first discovery of this in 1932 when they found that the Amazon molly *(P. formosa),* a species

125

normally ranging through the coastal and inland waters of northeastern Mexico and Texas, existed in nature only as a female population. The species was able to maintain itself by mating with males of other species occurring in the same area, such as *P. latipinna* and *P. sphenops*.

The live-bearing topminnows have long been popular with tropical fish hobbyists. Countless breeding experiments, both planned and haphazard, have resulted in many new domestic strains of these remarkable fishes. The lowly guppy serves as a good example: the wild form has a tail of moderate length, although that of the male is usually longer and more flowing than that of the female; many domestic tail varieties have been developed.

From the southeastern United States comes the world-famous mosquitofish *(Gambusia affinis)*. It is slightly larger than the guppy, with the adult females ranging between 2 and 3 inches and the males slightly smaller. Melanistic forms with erratic spotting are often found in this species. The ability of *Gambusia* to consume quantities of mosquito larvae and pupae makes it an item in demand in tropical and temperate areas where those pests abound. For this reason it has been imported into many areas where it does not normally occur.

One of the smallest of the active mosquitofishes is the least killifish *(Heterandria formosa)*: as an adult it is scarcely 1 inch in length. It is easily identified by the black band along the side of the body and the black spot at the base of the dorsal fin. *Heterandria* is found from North Carolina to Florida, and is more a mid-water fish than *Gambusia* and the other topminnows.

Mollies have long been favorites of the aquarists because of the male's beautiful, sail-like dorsal fin. The most common species in the southeastern United States is *Poecilia latipinna*, which reaches a length of about 4 inches and is found from South Carolina to Mexico in both fresh water and saltwater. Mottled blackish sailfin mollies sometimes occur in nature; in Florida they are most often found in sulphur springs. Aquarists have duplicated many of these melanistic forms and have also produced entirely black mollies. It may be noted that these black mollies have been produced not only from *P. latipinna* but also from other species such as *P. velifera* and *P. sphenops*.

In recent years six non-native poeciliids have become established in various localities in the United States and Canada.

Four-eyed Fishes (Family Anablepidae)

The Cuatro ojos or the four eyes is a well-known fish in many areas of southern

Mexico, Central America, and northern South America. Two species are recognized, both in the same genus, *Anableps;* they reach a normal maximum length of 6 to 8 inches, although some have been recorded at 12 inches.

The four-eyed fish spends much of its time cruising just below the surface of the water with the upper half of its eyes protruding. The water line is at the center of each eye, and at this point the eye is neatly divided by a longitudinal epithelial band so that the upper and lower portions are separate; hence the name "four eyes." Not only is the cornea divided, but *Anableps* carries this division a step further and has separate retinas in the backs of the eyes. An object out of water is seen through the upper eye and is brought to focus on the lower retina, whereas an object underwater is seen through the under cornea and is brought to focus on the upper retina. Air vision requires a different lens system than does underwater vision. *Anableps* solves this problem by having the lens of the eye oval-shaped so that an object viewed underwater is seen through a portion of the lens much thicker than the portion above the surface of the water.

Like other fishes resembling poeciliids, *Anableps* is viviparous, with the young being born alive. Like other fishes of this group, the anterior rays of the anal

Four-eyed fish (Anableps anableps); fresh-water.

fin are modified to serve as a phallic organ. Compared with other related fishes, then, there is nothing exceptional about their reproduction up to this point. However, we now come upon one of the most amazing reproductive patterns in the fish world. For coitus to take place, a "left-handed" male must always mate with a "right-handed" female, and a "right-handed" male with a "left-handed" female; to explain this, it should be noted that in some males the modified anal fin or intromittent organ is able to move only to the left and in others only to the right. The female has a similar peculiarity; her genital aperture is covered by a special scale which allows it to open on one side and not on the other.

Goodeids (Family Goodeidae)

In the highlands of Mexico and adjacent areas there is a group of about two dozen species of small fishes known as goodeids. They have a reproductive pattern intermediate between that of the egg-laying cyprinodont topminnows and the live-bearing poeciliid topminnows. Although the goodeids resemble the poeciliids in that they bear their young alive, they lack the highly developed gonopodium of the latter. Instead, the male goodeids have an anal fin that shows only a small amount of modification, with the first six rays set apart from the rest of the structure by a notch. The poeciliids and goodeids are further differentiated by the fact that the male goodeids are capable of fertilizing only one batch of eggs at a time, while the poeciliids fertilize several successive broods with one deposit of sperm.

Silversides (Family Atherinidae)

The atherinid silversides are often called smelts but are different from the osmerid or true smelts in that they have two separate dorsal fins, the first one of spines and the second of soft rays. In addition, there is a broad, silvery band along the sides and the lateral line is missing. The pelvic fins are usually in the center of the abdomen. The silversides are chiefly marine species found in tropical and temperate waters around the world; about 150 kinds are known.

One of the best-known silversides is the grunion (Leuresthes tenuis), a small, 5- to 7-inch shallow-water fish found along the shores of southern California and Baja California. Its peculiar spawning habits take it high on the beach at night during the period of the highest tides. Here the female wriggles into the sand, burying her eggs at a depth of 2 inches; at the same time, the male wraps himself around her on top of the sand and fertilizes the eggs. The grunions then flop back to the water and are carried out to deeper water by succeeding waves. The eggs remain in the sand until the next series of high tides, when they hatch within three minutes after the water first touches them. The spawning runs are correlated with the phases of the moon, usually occurring a day or two after each full or new moon. The grunion has a short life history, maturing at the age of one year and seldom surviving beyond three years.

In the eastern part of the United States there are several fresh- and brackish-water silversides, such as the 4-inch brook silverside *(Labidesthes sicculus)*, a form that ranges from the Great Lakes to Florida and Texas. Marine species that enter fresh water include the tidewater silverside *(Menidia beryllina)*, whereas the Mississippi silverside *(M. audens)* is restricted to fresh water.

In the fresh waters of Mexico there are a fair number of species of *Chirostoma*, most of them important market fishes; they reach a length of about 20 inches and are characterized by a jutting lower jaw.

SQUIRRELFISHES AND THEIR RELATIVES
(Order Beryciformes)

In some respects this is a transitional group of fishes, intermediate between the primitive forms that have fins with few or no spines and the more advanced, typically perchlike, spiny-rayed species described under the order Perciformes. The group is characterized internally by several obscure anatomical similarities and externally by the fact that the soft dorsal fin is preceded by a series of spiny rays and the many-rayed pelvic fins are thoracic in position—that is, placed just behind the pectoral fins. Most of the twelve families are deep-sea groups, and many of them are bright red in color.

Squirrelfishes and Soldierfishes (Family Holocentridae)

Bright colors—usually some shade of red—and shallow-water tropical reefs are invariably associated with the nocturnal squirrelfishes. In the daytime they tend to hide in crevices and cracks, and they move out over the reefs at night to forage. These fishes are noted for their sharp spines and sharp scales as well as their large squirrel-like eyes.

Although the squirrelfishes have a worldwide distribution in tropical marine waters, the total number of species is only around seventy. As adults, squirrelfishes tend to remain near the bottom in one general area. The larval fishes become a part of the floating plankton and are apt to be swept many miles away by surface currents, after which they settle to the bottom.

The genus *Holocentrus* is the largest genus in the family; these fishes can be recognized by their strong preopercular spine and very long, dagger-like anal spine, one of four spines preceding the soft rays of the fin. The 12-inch longspine squirrelfish *(H. rufus)* is a common tropical Atlantic form.

The second largest genus in the family is *Myripristis*, a group sometimes called soldierfishes. In Hawaii, they are known as menpachi and command a premium market price. The 8-inch blackbar soldierfish *(M. jacobus)* occurs on both sides of the Atlantic and in the Americas from Florida and the Bahamas to southeastern Brazil. Isopod crustaceans are frequently attached to this species.

Alfonsinos (Family Berycidae)

The deep-water alfonsinos are often brightly colored and are among the most primitive of the beryciform fishes. The 24-inch red *Beryx splendens*, one of the most common species, is of worldwide distribution. Its usual depth range is between 1,800 and 2,400 feet. The alfonsinos resemble the squirrelfishes but have a shorter, stumpy body with a very much elongated caudal peduncle.

DORIES, BOARFISHES, AND THEIR RELATIVES (Order Zeiformes)

The enigmatic deep-sea zeomorphs are a small group of spiny-rayed fishes, usually thin and deep-bodied, that have long presented ichthyologists with classification problems that even today are not entirely solved. They usually have enormously distensible jaws, set at an oblique angle, and pelvic fins with six to nine rays. Two of the six families in the order will be considered.

Dories (Family Zeidae)

Unlike most of the other zeomorph fishes, which are deep-sea forms, the pouting john dories are mid-water species, found at depths that can easily be fished with commercial gear. These fishes are readily identified by the large round black spot surrounded by a yellow ring that is located in the center of the body. As the fish grows, the spinous dorsal of some ten rays develops long, trailing

Longspine squirrelfish (Holocentrus rufus); Atlantic marine.

filaments that may extend almost to the end of the tail fin. Identification is further aided by the presence of a number of small spines or bucklers along the bases of both the dorsal and anal fins. There is also a series of eight or nine spinous plates along the abdomen.

The American john dory *(Zenopsis ocellata)* is most often caught along the continental shelf from Nova Scotia to North Carolina; the maximum size for the species is 2 feet and 7 pounds. It is not a commercially important species, although its European counterpart *(Z. faber)* is a valued food item. The mirror dory *(Z. nebulosa)* is the Pacific American species.

Boarfishes (Family Caproidae)

These are bright red fishes that can often be recognized by the extreme depth of the slim body. The horizontal distance from the snout to the end of the caudal peduncle is usually equal to the vertical distance from the base of the dorsal fin to the bottom of the abdomen; thus, in profile, the boarfish usually forms a rhomboid or diamond. Another distinguishing feature is the presence of three anal spines entirely separate from the soft rays of the anal fin and not attached to them. The deepbody boarfish *(Antigonia capros)* is a widely distributed species known from many parts of the Atlantic and the western Pacific.

OPAH AND RIBBONFISHES (Order Lampridiformes)

There is a considerable variation in appearance among the members of this rare, deep-water group of marine fishes; however, they all have soft-rayed fins and protrusible jaws of a type not found among other fishes. Six families are recognized.

Opah (Family Lamprididae)

The opah *(Lampris regius)*, sometimes called the moonfish, is the only member of its family; it reachs a length of 6 feet and a weight of almost 600 pounds. Its food consists chiefly of squids, octopuses, and crustaceans. The body is oval-shaped and laterally compressed, with a spectacular color pattern: blue to gray above, changing to rose red on the undersurface, with white spots covering the entire body. The flesh of the opah has an excellent flavor.

Although the opah occurs in all seas, large numbers of them are found only in the Tokyo wholesale fish market, where Japanese fishing boats from all over the world bring their catches. Japanese tuna long-line boats operating on the high seas often catch opahs at depths ranging from 400 to 1,000 feet.

Ribbonfishes, Oarfishes, and Crestfishes (Families Trachipteridae, Regalecidae, and Lophotidae)

These are fragile, offshore, usually deep-water species that are quite spectacular anatomically. The body is very thin; for example, a ribbonfish 7 feet long might have a body 12 inches deep and only 2 inches (or even less) wide. The dorsal fin usually starts on top of the head as a plumelike topknot and extends down the long body to the tail fin, which is quite long and at a right angle to the body. Actually, this is the upper lobe of the tail fin, the lower lobe being undeveloped. As the juvenile fish grows, the topknot usually decreases in size, and the right-angled tail breaks, with the remaining portion coming to lie more in line with the body. The pelvic fins, originally quite large, decrease in size and may even be lost during this growth process. These radical growth changes explain why so many supposedly different species of these fishes have been described.

The largest of the three families of ribbon-like fishes is the Trachipteridae, with five species known from the United States and Canada. The king-of-the-salmon *(Trachipterus altivelis)* and the dealfish *(T. arcticus)* are noted members of this family. The 22-foot oarfish *(Regalecus glesne)* is assigned to a separate family, Regalecidae, chiefly on the basis of the very elongate, oarlike pelvic fins. The third family, Lophotidae, includes the crestfishes, a scaleless group of ribbon-like species that retain the anal fin but lack the pelvic fins.

TUBE-MOUTHED FISHES (Order Gasterosteiformes)

Five of the eight families of tube-mouthed fishes are found in North America. In addition to the tubelike snout, characteristics exhibited by various families within the order include a complete or partial external armor in the form of bony plates, a special external pouch for the incubation of eggs, a primitive kidney, and tufted, lobelike gills.

Sticklebacks (Family Gasterosteidae)

Several of the dozen species in the stickleback family live as easily in fresh water

*Nest-building and courtship. American sticklebacks show variations of the
15-spine stickleback (Spinachia spinachia) pattern. The male builds the nest
and "sews" it together by secreting a binding thread.*

as in brackish water or saltwater. Most sticklebacks are armored with a series
of bony plates along the sides of the body; the number of these plates depends
upon the species as well as the temperature and salinity of the water, and ranges
up to thirty-six. Because of the spines, the plates on the sides, and the very
narrow caudal peduncle, identification is not difficult.

With the onset of the breeding season, usually in the spring of the year, the
male stickleback develops a bright red undersurface and assumes his role as the
more active member of the mating pair. His first breeding activity is the con-
struction of a nest, using as a base the leafy stems of aquatic plants. The nest is
held together by a threadlike material secreted from a section of the kidney,
which becomes specially modified for this purpose during the breeding season.
The male usually swims around the nest several times while paying out this
binding thread. Then by such actions as nipping at the female's fins, chasing
her, and doing a courtship dance, he entices or drives her to lay her eggs in this
leafy bower. After she has deposited the eggs, she often leaves, by burrowing
a hole through the bottom of the nest. The male, noted for his solicitous care

He then drives the pregnant female into the nest by attacking her and biting her tail.

of the eggs and the young, then moves into the nest and spews milt over the eggs, ensuring adequate fertilization. This process may subsequently be repeated with several different females, and some males may even have several nests at the same time. Aeration of the eggs during the six-day incubation period is achieved by the male's swimming around the nest and vigorously fanning the eggs with his pectoral fins. After the eggs have hatched, the male still maintains a watch over the youngsters and attempts to keep them in the area of the nest.

Two of the sticklebacks are very widely distributed: the threespine stickleback *(Gasterosteus aculeatus)* occurs throughout most of the northern hemisphere in both salt and fresh water, and the ninespine stickleback *(Pungitius pungitius)* has a similar distribution but is a more polar species that does not range much farther south than New Jersey or central Europe.

The brook stickleback *(Culaea inconstans)* is a small, 2.5-inch fresh-water species found in cold waters from the latitude of Ohio northward to that of northern British Columbia and Quebec. It may be identified by the four to six, usually five, spines in front of the dorsal. The fourspine stickleback *(Apeltes quadracus*) is a common species along the eastern American seaboard from Nova Scotia to Virginia.

The slender 6.5-inch tube-snout *(Aulorhynchus flavidus)* is a marine species ranging from southern California to Alaska. In some areas it is so abundant that it serves as a forage fish for other species; it is often found in the stomachs of larger carnivorous fishes. The tube-snout looks much like a stickleback with two extra inches of length added to the center of the body; there are about twenty-five spines in front of the soft dorsal fin instead of the fifteen or fewer found in the other sticklebacks. In aquarium work we have found the tube-snout to be extremely susceptible to shock. Of a netful brought into an aquarium tank, about half will go into either temporary shock or a permanent shock that eventually causes death.

Cornetfishes (Family Fistulariidae)

The cornetfishes, sometimes called flutemouths, are fairly common in tropical seas, especially around reefs, where they swim about in loosely formed schools. There are about five species, at least one of which, the bluespotted cornetfish *(Fistularia tabacaria)*, reaches a length of 6 feet. Because of its slender body, it weighs only around 7.5 pounds at this length. The principal identifying mark of the cornetfish is a long, flexible filament extending from the center of the tail fin. Almost as long as the filament is the fish's tubular snout, which is one of the most efficient food pipettes known in the fish world.

Trumpetfishes (Family Aulostomidae)

The trumpetfish looks much like the cornetfish but lacks the long filament on the end of the tail and is further distinguished by a series of isolated spines in front of the dorsal fin. Maximum length for any of the four species is around 2 feet. These fishes are often found on the same tropical reef as cornetfishes, but they are not nearly as common and are often difficult to locate because of their ability to camouflage themselves. The common Atlantic species is *Aulostomus maculatus*.

Snipefishes (Family Macrorhamphosidae)

The snipefishes, sometimes called bellows fishes, are a small group of about eleven species divided among four genera. They are deep-bodied fishes with a long snout and a single, very long dorsal fin spine that extends backward toward the tail. Characteristically there are two series of bony plates on each side of the back, forming an imperfect exoskeleton. All species are small, none being more than 10 inches long. They are found in tropical and temperate marine zones ranging from moderate depths to deep water. Two species occur in North American waters, the Atlantic longspine snipefish *(Macrorhamphosus scolopax)* and the slender snipefish *(M. gracilis)*, which is found both in the Atlantic and in the Pacific.

Pipefishes and Seahorses (Family Syngnathidae)

The Pacific giant seahorse *(Hippocampus ingens)* was originally described from San Diego in 1858. Although not uncommon farther south in the American tropics as far as Ecuador, it virtually disappeared from the United States until 1963, when it appeared again in its former haunts. Its disappearance and return after more than a century still remain an ichthyological mystery. On the Atlantic coast, the lined seahorse *(H. erectus)* is usually present in sufficient abundance in the Florida Keys for fish jobbers to ship it to aquarium outlets around the United States. In summer this same species ranges as far north as Long Island, but in winter it disappears from these northern areas.

The 1.5-inch dwarf seahorse *(H. zosterae)*, found from eastern Florida to Campeche, has been sold unscrupulously by promoters to gullible prospective aquarists as an easy way to get into tropical marine fish-keeping. There is no easy way; nevertheless, this delightful horse has abilities not possessed by the other approximately two dozen seahorse members of the family. It survives under a wide variety of salinity and temperature conditions, which in itself is significant; and on top of that, it reproduces in captivity with an ease unmatched by any other seahorse.

The chubby seahorses have pencil-like relatives long recognized as pipefishes. The male pipefish, like the seahorse, incubates the young in a brood pouch usually located under the tail, although there are a few belly-pouch forms. Seahorses have a sealed pouch that opens through a small port just behind the anal fin, whereas pipefishes have a slit like pouch opening from one end to the other.

The pipefish and seahorse family has a number of anatomical peculiarities, foremost of which is a secondary or outside bony skeleton arranged in a series

137

of plates forming rings. The gills are tufted, and there is a primitive kidney. The family is a small one of not more than 170 species. In American waters there are twenty-six pipefishes in the Atlantic and eleven in the Pacific.

Most pipefishes and seahorses are shallow-water forms living among eelgrass or other vegetation, and sometimes among coral. One of the most common eelgrass forms occurring from Nova Scotia to Florida is the northern pipefish *(Syngnathus fuscus);* a similar but smaller species, the gulf pipefish *(S. scovelli)* takes over the same habitat from Florida to Yucatan. Floating weed serves as the habitat for the sargassum pipefish *(S. pelagicus).* The most secretive member of the family is undoubtedly the 2-inch Bahaman finless pipefish *(Penetopteryx nanus),* which apparently spends its time hiding in the interstices of red organ-pipe coral. The largest American Atlantic pipefish is the 14-inch bull pipefish *(S. springeri),* which is usually found at depths of 60 to 420 feet. The largest Pacific species is the kelp pipefish *(S. californiensis),* which reaches 23 inches.

SWAMP EELS (Order Synbranchiformes)

This strange assemblage of some eight species of swamp eels is characterized by the fact that these fishes are air-breathers and not true eels. They lack the paired fins—the pelvic and pectoral fins—and the dorsal and anal fins are reduced to a ridge. They are found in tropical fresh and brackish waters of Africa, Asia, the Indo-Australian archipelago and from Mexico to South America; there is one marine species in the Malay Peninsula. The arrangement of the gills and gill openings varies widely in the different species, so that according to some specialists several families of swamp eels should be recognized rather than the single family Synbranchidae.

The 2-foot-6-inch rice eel *(Monopterus albus)* occurs in fresh water through-out Southeast Asia, the Philippines, and Indonesia. In many areas it is used as food. In recent years it has been introduced in the Hawaiian Islands and has become established there. Like the lungfish, the rice eel is able to survive in deep mud pockets during the dry season when the water in the ponds dries up.

The principal American representative of this group is the wide-ranging *Synbranchus marmoratus,* found from Yucatán to Patagonia, which may reach a length of 3 to 5 feet. This burrowing nocturnal species has four well-developed gills and may be identified by the single gill opening under the head. It has a blind relative, *Furmastix infernalis,* known from a single 12.75-inch specimen from a Yucatán cave.

Top: Trumpetfish (Aulostomus maculatus); Atlantic marine.
Bottom: Lined seahorse (Hippocampus erectus); Atlantic marine.

PERCHLIKE FISHES (Order Perciformes)

This is the largest order of fishes, containing more than 8,000 species in some 156 families. Considerable anatomical variation exists among the twenty subordinal groups, some of the more important of which are discussed here.

Snooks (Family Centropomidae)

All members of the centropomid family have a lateral line running out to the end of the tail. The family includes large fishes highly prized by commercial and sport fishermen, and small species that are popular with aquarists. An example of the large species is the Atlantic marine common snook *(Centropomus undecimalis)*. Small aquarium species are well represented by the transparent, brackish-water Asiatic glassfishes, formerly known as ambassids, such as *Chanda ranga*. Also included in this small family is the fabulous Nile perch *(Lates niloticus)*, which attains a weight of 200 pounds, as well as several other similar African fresh-water game fishes.

The shovel-headed snooks are a group of about eight species found along both sides of the tropical Atlantic as well as in the tropical eastern Pacific. They readily enter rivers and swim upstream into entirely fresh water. The most common snook of Florida *(C. undecimalis)* is found in greatest abundance in mangrove areas and is a relatively sedentary fish. From 28 to 30 pounds is their average size, although they have been known to reach 50.5 pounds and a length of 56 inches.

Sea Basses and Groupers (Family Serranidae)

Among the approximately 400 species in this family we find many of the world's most important food fishes, as well as a few that have been known to cause tropical fish poisoning, or ciguatera. The size rage of these fishes is extraordinary, some species maturing at slightly more than 1 inch in length, others maturing at about 4 feet at weights of about 50 pounds, and a few eventually reaching weights of 1,000 pounds. The majority of these fishes are carnivorous, and have large mouths and sharp teeth. A number of species spend their time sitting on the bottom waiting for prey; some are roamers. Serranids are most abundant in tropical seas, somewhat less abundant in temperate waters, and do not occur at all in the Arctic or the Antarctic.

Reproductive patterns among the serranids show a number of variables. Some species are born as females, and then later a few or all become functional males. Self-fertilization is normal for some species, with an individual containing both eggs and sperm. However, for most hermaphroditic species spawning is a group affair, with the result that cross-fertilization is normal and inbreeding minimized.

The large genus *Epinephelus* includes a great number of spotted and mottled groupers. Some, such as the giant Atlantic jewfish *(E. itajara)*, may weigh as much as 750 pounds. Another, the Nassau grouper *(E. striatus)*, has the reputation of being so friendly that diving photographers sometimes find it difficult to keep it far enough away to take pictures of it. The Atlantic hamlets of the genus *Hypoplectrus* are a most colorful group, with the common names indicating their color, such as the blue, yellowfin, indigo, butter, and black hamlets.

Mycteroperca is another important group of large serranids including such interesting species as the Pacific broomtail grouper *(M. xenarcha)* and the Atlantic tiger grouper *(M. tigris)*. Along the California coasts the kelp and sand basses of the genus *Paralabrax* are important sport fishes.

Soapfishes (Family Grammistidae)

The soapfishes are a peculiar group of fishes resembling sea basses. They are most efficient at hiding, and many may be living in an area without divers being aware of them. As the result of any activity—such as thrashing about or being handled—their body mucus creates a soapsuds effect in the water or on the hands of anyone handling them. The mucus has an acrid taste, and it has been postulated that each species of soapfish has its own kind of mucus. The greater soapfish *(Rypticus saponaceus)* is a mottled, 12-inch, inshore species found on both sides of the Atlantic. Its cousin in the Pacific American coastal areas is the Mexican soapfish *(R. bicolor)*.

The name of the family, Grammistidae, is derived from the generic name of the golden-striped grouper *(Grammistes sexlineatus)*, an attractive Indo-Pacific aquarium species known for its bitter mucus. There are about thirty species of the grammistid family in shallow tropical and temperate seas.

Temperate Basses (Family Percichthyidae)

Only recently (in 1966) has this offshoot of the serranid sea basses been recognized as a distinct family. Their separation from the serranids is based on a large

Overleaf, left: Nassau grouper (Epinephelus striatus); Atlantic marine. Right, top to bottom: Pacific creole (Paranthias colonius); Pacific marine. Snook (Centropomus undecimalis); Atlantic marine. Blue hamlet (Hypoplectrus gemma); Atlantic marine.

number of internal anatomical differences; externally they may be identified by a single main spine on the opercle and a forked caudal fin. By contrast, serranid sea basses have an extra spine or flat opercular point below the main spine, and the caudal fin is usually rounded, lunate, or truncate.

Although many groupers and sea basses spend much time sitting on the bottom, the striped bass *(Morone saxatilis)* is usually on the move; this trait undoubtedly contributes to its popularity as a sport fish. Its original distribution was along the American Atlantic coast from the Gulf of St. Lawrence to northern Florida. In 1879 and 1882 two shipments totaling 432 fish were transported to California and planted in the San Francisco area; in less than ten years the striped bass in this region had mushroomed to such an extent that a commercial fishery for them was established. Today the fish is found on the American west coast from the state of Washington to southern California. Stripers move into fresh water for spawning; this change of habitat usually takes place in the spring of the year.

The 10-inch white perch *(M. americana)* has a slightly heavier body than the striped bass, and lacks the stripes. This brackish-water species ranges from the Gulf of St. Lawrence to South Carolina and may occasionally be landlocked in fresh-water lakes.

The wreckfish *(Polyprion americanus)* may be found as deep as 1,800 feet. This 100-pound, 6-foot fish occurs on both sides of the tropical and temperate Atlantic, but is more common on the European coasts than on the American coasts. Other American species include the fresh-water white and yellow basses *(M. chrysops* and *M. mississippiensis)* and the Pacific giant sea bass *(Stereolepis gigas)*.

Basslets *(Family Grammidae)*

This small group of about nine tropical sea bass relatives is noted for spectacular colors. Grammid basslets are distinguished from the serranid sea basses by several anatomical differences: the lateral line present in the sea basses is interrupted or absent in the basslets; the number of dorsal fin spines is greater than in the sea basses; and the pelvic fins have one spine and five soft rays. The 3-inch violet and orange fairy basslet *(Gramma loreto)* has proved very popular with aquarists. It ranges from Bermuda and the Bahamas to Venezuela but does not occur in Florida. Depth preference ranges all the way from shallow water to 190 feet.

Top: Giant sea bass (Stereolepis gigas); Pacific marine.
Bottom: Walleye (Stizostedion vitreum); fresh-water.

Aholeholes (Family Kuhliidae)

The aholeholes are silvery, tropical Indo-Pacific fishes that look much like the North American fresh-water sunfishes (family Centrarchidae). Fewer than a dozen species are known. The majority are marine, but they move readily into brackish water, and a few are entirely fresh-water in habitat. They may range in size up to 18 inches. The attractive 8-inch flagtail *(Kuhlia taeniura)*, with its five black longitudinal stripes across the tail, is one of the most distinctive. It ranges east across the Pacific to Mexico.

Sunfishes (Family Centrarchidae)

"Largemouth bass," "bluegill," and "crappie" are names that are very familiar to the American fresh-water angler. About thirty kinds of sunfishes are recognized. All of them were originally North American fishes, but several species, including the bluegill and the largemouth, have been introduced into Europe and elsewhere. Typically, in sunfishes the spiny-rayed and soft-rayed portions of the dorsal fin are continuous, and in some species, such as the largemouth basses, there is a notch between the two sections; in the related perch family, Percidae, the two fins are entirely separate. Some of the species of sunfishes are so similar that it is difficult to distinguish between them; this is especially true of the juveniles. The small species of centrarchids are well known to aquarists. The beautiful, 3.5-inch bluespotted sunfish *(Enneacanthus gloriosus)* is a common species through the eastern and southern areas of the United States. Two other striking pygmy sunfishes—the banded *Elassoma zonatum*, found in the central United States, and the mottled *E. evergladei*, found in Florida—are both sexually mature at a length of 1 inch and never grow larger than 1.5 inches. The 3-inch blackbanded sunfish *(Enneacanthus chaetodon)*, which is common from New Jersey to northern Florida, is another attractive species. Strangely, this fish is bred extensively in Germany and shipped to countries all over the world, including the United States. Apparently it is easier to do this than to collect it from its normal habitat.

The sunfishes are nest-builders. The male, using his tail as a fan, hollows out a small depression in the sand; then he entices a receptive female to the nest, where she lays her eggs and he fertilizes them. After the eggs are laid, he jealously guards the nest, chasing off the female and aggressively attacking any intruder.

Preceding pages, top left: Bluegill sunfish (Lepomis macrochirus); fresh-water. Bottom left: Candy basslet (Liopropoma carmabi); Atlantic marine. Top right: Blackbanded sunfish (Enneacanthus chaetodon); fresh-water. Bottom right: Fairy basslet (Gramma loreto); Atlantic marine.

Sunfishes can sometimes be identified by the nature of the ear lobe, the small extension of the opercle just above the pectoral fin. On the longear sunfish *(Lepomis megalotis)*, the edge of the very long ear flap is rimmed with white, and the ear flap is often covered with orange dots or flushed with a reddish color. The pumpkinseed *(L. gibbosus)* has a large, blood-red blotch on the end of the ear flap.

The largemouth bass *(Micropterus salmoides)* is the largest species in the family, with specimens reported at 25 pounds; the official angler record, however, is somewhat less: 22.5 pounds for a largemouth measuring 32.5 inches. The largest recorded weight for the smallmouth *(M. dolomieui)* is almost 12 pounds for a 27-inch fish. These larger centrarchids often feed upon smaller ones; consequently, normal stocking practice is to introduce with them such smaller forage fishes as the bluegill *(Lepomis macrochirus)*.

The bluegill is usually found in the still water of lakes and ponds where vegetation is present. The dark blotch on the posterior base of the soft dorsal fin and the five to seven vertical bars across the body are reliable identifying marks. The bluegill usually becomes mature at 3.5 inches but may reach a length of 15 inches and a weight of 4.75 pounds.

The two species of crappies originally occurred only in the eastern part of the United States, but because of their popularity with sport fishermen, they have been widely planted in many waters across North America. The white crappie *(Pomoxis annularis)* is usually found in turbid rivers, lakes, and sloughs, whereas the black crappie *(P. nigromaculatus)* prefers clear water. Although 12 inches is a respectable length for either of the two species, specimens ranging between 19 and 21 inches in length and weighing about 5 pounds have been caught.

The only centrarchid sunfish originally occurring in the western part of the United States—although others have been introduced—is the Sacramento perch *(Archoplites interruptus)*, found in California's Sacramento and San Joaquin basins; most of the fish of this species are less than 1 foot in length.

Perches, Walleyes, and Darters (Family Percidae)

The familiar yellow perch *(Perca flavescens)* is a small, shallow-water fish found in lakes, ponds, and slow-moving streams. Like all American members of the family, it originally occurred in North America east of the Rockies only, but subsequently was widely introduced elsewhere. Although always popular with youngsters and with the casual fisherman, it has had an erratic history as a food fish.

The yellow perch is easily recognized by the six to nine blackish bars on the sides of the body; the young are silvery in background color, but as they become mature they develop a brassy or golden body color with orange ventral and anal fins. A 15-inch perch weighing slightly more than 1 pound is considered a large fish, but the record is held by a fish that was caught in 1865 and weighed 4.5 pounds. Spawning takes place in the spring, the eggs being laid at night in long strings usually found affixed to shallow-water vegetation. A single female perch has been known to deposit a string of eggs 81 inches in length, and a string may contain from 10,000 to 48,000 eggs, depending on the size of the fish.

The perches make up one of the three subfamilies into which the family is divided. The second group, of which there are a few representatives in both Europe and North America, contains the walleyes, the saugers, and the pike perches. The third and largest group contains the smallest species, the darters, more than 110 of which have been described, all from North America.

The 3-foot walleye *(Stizostedion vitreum)*, sometimes also called the pike perch, has a mottled pattern, usually with a large black blotch at the posterior end of the spinous dorsal fin; it also has many small canine teeth. This fish is quite popular with sport fishermen throughout its range in eastern North America and has been a valuable commercial species in Lake Erie. The blue walleye and the yellow walleye are recognized geographic varieties of the common walleye.

The sauger *(S. canadense)* resembles the walleye but has a spotted spiny dorsal fin without the black blotch at the base. It is a smaller fish than the walleye; the anglers' world record is an 8.25-pound fish with a length of 30 inches.

Darters are small, quick, bottom-dwelling fishes found in a variety of habitats but limited to temperate North America east of the Rocky Mountains. Most of them are less than 4 inches in length, and the largest reaches only 9 inches. Although some have distinctive markings, a specialist is often needed for a certain identification. Among the darters are found some of the most brilliantly colored fishes in North America; this is especially true during the breeding season, when their colors are greatly enhanced. Some darters distribute their eggs indiscriminately; but others, such as the 2.5-inch johnny darter *(Etheostoma nigrum)*, lay their eggs under a rock or in a small cave while in an upside-down position; the male then aerates, cleans, and guards the eggs for about three weeks until they hatch. Other darters, who do not guard the eggs, may lay them

Top: Short bigeye (Pristigenys alta); Atlantic marine.
Bottom: Blackfin cardinalfish (Astrapogon puncticulatus); Atlantic marine.

Sharksucker (Echeneis naucrates) attached to loggerhead turtle; worldwide

on plants, on the bottom, or may bury them. The johnny darter is a representative of the largest genus of darters, *Etheostoma*, which has some eighty species assigned to it.

Bigeyes (Family Priacanthidae)

Very large eyes, small rough scales, and bright red color, rarely with a pattern, are the marks of the carnivorous, nocturnal bigeyes, sometimes called catalufas. The attachment of the inner ventral fin to the abdomen by a broad membrane is also a good identifying feature. Fewer than eighteen species are recognized, but some of these are very widely distributed. They are bottom-dwelling marine fishes, usually found in deeper water than the squirrelfishes, which they resemble. Their maximum size is about 2 feet. The common bigeye *(Priacanthus arenatus)* is a representative species; it attains a length of 14 inches and is found on both sides of the temperate and tropical Atlantic. The Pacific species is the popeye catalufa *(Pristigenys serrula)*.

Sharksucker (Echeneis naucrates), showing sucking disk; worldwide marine.

Cardinalfishes (Family Apogonidae)

Many of the cardinals are attractively patterned and often brightly colored; shades of brown or red are common, as in the barred cardinalfish *(Apogon binotatus)*, a tropical Atlantic species. Most of the species are small, tropical marine fishes, with the majority less than 4 inches in length. The largest cardinalfishes are 6 to 8 inches long and are brackish-water species living in mangrove swamps. Cardinalfishes usually occur in shallow water, but there are a few species found only in deep water. Two separate dorsal fins and two instead of the usual three anal spines are the identifying features of the family. Many of the species are mouthbrooders; in some it is only the male that takes the eggs into the mouth for incubation; in others, only the female; and in still others, it is suspected that both the male and female incubate the eggs. Some cardinal males are described as picking up the eggs and holding them in the mouth only while danger threatens.

There are about twenty North American Atlantic shallow-water cardinalfishes, most of which occur in the Bahamas and Florida. Only one Pacific species, the Guadalupe cardinalfish *(A. guadalupensis)*, reaches southern California.

One of the most interesting cardinalfishes is the conchfish *(Astrapogon stellatus)*: as many as five of these fish may live at one time in the mantle cavity of a single 10-inch queen conch, moving out at night to feed.

Tilefishes (Family Branchiostegidae)

Most of the fifteen or so species of tilefishes, sometimes called blanquillos, are very elongated and small—usually less than 2 feet in length—and have many-rayed dorsal and anal fins. They are primarily tropical marine species, but a few move into temperate waters. There is one well-known member of the family: the strange tilefish *(Lopholatilus chamaeleonticeps)*, a large, beautiful blue deep-water fish that in the past has occurred in fluctuating abundance off the American Atlantic coast. It was first discovered in 1879, and almost immediately aroused considerable interest in its possibilities for commercial fishery. Unfortunately, just as the fishery was getting started, in 1882, millions of tilefishes ranging up to 50 pounds in weight were found dead, floating at the surface over thousands of square miles of the offshore Atlantic coast. This tremendous mortality was apparently due to a temperature change, but afterward the tilefish could no longer be caught in their old haunts. Scientists speculated for a time that the species might be extinct, but it gradually returned to its former abundance until, by 1916, some 11,500,000 pounds were marketed. Since then, however, the commercial demand for the tilefish has declined.

The graceful, 2-foot American Atlantic sand tilefish *(Malacanthus plumieri)* builds its own burrow, into which it retreats head first with the approach of danger. On the Pacific coast the ocean whitefish *(Caulolatilus princeps)* ranges from the Gulf of California to Washington, although it is rare north of Point Conception; its yellowish fins give it a most attractive appearance when it is swimming.

Bluefish (Family Pomatomidae)

The bloodthirsty feeding habits of the bluefish *(Pomatomus saltatrix)* remind one of the South American piranha. Even when these fish have eaten their fill, they continue to slaughter more fish, seemingly for the pure love of killing.

The bluefish is a fast-moving, schooling marine species, found in tropical and temperate waters around the world with the exception of the central and eastern Pacific. Its movements up and down the American Atlantic coast are to a certain extent correlated with those of the schools of menhaden and other fish on which it feeds. The species reaches a maximum weight of 27 pounds, but even in the 5- to 10-pound range the bluefish is a favorite of the saltwater angler, not only because of its fighting qualities, but also because it is good to eat. There is an identifying black blotch at the base of the pectoral fin. This is the only species known.

Cobia (Family Rachycentridae)

The fast-moving, voracious cobia *(Rachycentron canadum)* is easily identified by the three dark stripes on the sides of the body. It is a large, streamlined fish that reaches a weight of 102 pounds and a length of almost 6 feet. There is only one species, which is worldwide in tropical and subtropical seas. In appearance the young cobia is very similar to the sharksucker, or remora; because of this similarity, it has been thought that the two kinds of fishes may be related. In the shark channel at the Miami Seaquarium, the cobias swim side by side with the large sharks, each of which has one or more sharksuckers attached to it.

Remoras or Sharksuckers (Family Echeneidae)

Shark fishermen sometimes receive an unexpected bonus in the form of small fishes known as remoras, or sharksuckers, which are attached to the sharks by a sucking disk located on the top of the head. As the shark is pulled on board, the sharksucker will either drop off into the water or flop onto the deck. Examination of the sucking disk reveals a series of 10 to 28 pairs of cross ridges, the number depending upon the species; each ridge is a modification of a spiny ray of the first dorsal fin. Although remoras are most often found attached to sharks, they may use other kinds of animals, or small boats and ships, as attachment surfaces. They have even been found inside the gill cavities of large manta rays and ocean sunfishes. There is one type, *Remilegia australis*, the whalesucker, which is usually found attached to whales of various species. Recent investigations have shown that some remoras feed on parasitic crustaceans attached to the host; in this regard, they may function somewhat like the cleaner fishes described earlier. The approximately eight species in the family have a wide

distribution through all tropical and temperate seas. The largest species is the striped, 36-inch *Echeneis naucrates*, which uses sharks as hosts; the smallest species is the 7-inch *Remoropsis pallidus*, which prefers tunas and swordfishes.

Jacks, Scads, and Pompanos (Family Carangidae)

Carangids vary greatly in shapes and sizes, but most of them have one thing in common—they move with great speed. Because of this, they provide a treat for the fisherman who hooks one on his line. As a group, they are excellent market fishes, with some, such as the pompanos, bringing premium prices. They occur around the world in tropical and temperate seas, and a few move readily into fresh water. Most of the 200 or so species have a blunt-headed, jacklike appearance that usually makes them easily recognizable. Along the sides of the caudal peduncle, just ahead of the tail, most species have a sharp ridge formed by a series of bony scutes, or plates; in some species these may extend along the entire lateral line. The popular crevalle jack *(Caranx hippos)*, ranging up to 70 pounds, is an example of a worldwide species found on the Atlantic coast from Nova Scotia to Uruguay.

A different body form is found in the slender, cigar-shaped species of the genus *Decapterus*, represented on the Atlantic coast by the round scad *(D. punctatus)* and on the Pacific by the Mexican scad *(D. hypodus)*. A similar body profile is characteristic of the commercially important Pacific jack mackerel *(Trachurus symmetricus)*.

There are some species, such as the amberjacks, that lack scutes on the lateral line; a typical example of this is the Atlantic *Seriola dumerili*. Some of the amberjacks have very attractive juvenile forms with brilliant golden bands, which are lost as the fish grows. Like its Atlantic cousin, the California yellow-tail *(S. dorsalis)* lacks the scutes on the sides of the caudal peduncle, but does have a small ridge in this area.

The beautiful, deep-bodied pompanos are graceful fishes when swimming. The 18-inch common Florida pompano *(Trachinotus carolinus)* is a valuable food species on the Atlantic coasts of the Americas. The threadfishes of the genus *Alectis* are always sure to attract attention because of the long streamers extending out from the first rays of both the dorsal and anal fins; as these fishes grow, the body proportions change considerably and the streamers shorten, so that the adult is sometimes quite different from the juvenile. The threadfishes are typically inshore species, whereas the other carangids range

Bar jack (Caranx ruber); Atlantic marine.   157

offshore. Other common carangids include the leatherjackets of the genera *Scomberoides* and *Oligoplites*, which are sometimes so abundant in tropical waters that it is impossible for a baited hook to reach the bottom without being taken by one or more of these fishes.

The lookdown *(Selene vomer)*, which ranges across the Atlantic, has a most bizarre appearance in that the eye is placed high on the large head at an inordinate distance from the mouth, giving the fish a supercilious look.

The 3.5-foot rainbow runner *(Elagatis bipinnulata)*, found throughout the tropics, is a cigar-shaped fish with a brilliant blue color on the back; along the side of the body there is a yellow stripe bordered below by a thin blue stripe. The presence of two small finlets, one after the second dorsal and one after the anal fin, is helpful in identification.

Old-time mariners tell us that the legendary pilot fish *(Naucrates ductor)* will lead lost swimmers, ships, or even whales to safety. Actually, they do not do a great deal of leading, although they are often found around sharks and other large fishes, as well as ships—in fact, wherever scraps of food are easily available.

Some of the carangids, both in the Atlantic and in the Pacific, have been found responsible for ciguatera, or tropical fish poisoning.

Dolphins *(Family Coryphaenidae)*

The name "dolphin" is often confusing, for it is applied to both a fish and an aquatic mammal. The spectacular dolphin fish is a tropical offshore sport species capable of swimming as fast as 37 miles an hour. Known as mahimahi in Hawaiian waters, it is the water-breathing *Coryphaena hippurus*, which reaches a length of five feet; the mammal is an air-breathing cetacean or porpoise of which a number of species are known. The fish has a long fin with as many as 65 rays extending down the back; it also has a forked tail and beautiful bluish color that is lost very quickly after the fish is captured. The adult male has a decidedly squarish head and may weigh as much as 67 pounds, whereas the female has a more rounded head and seldom weighs more than 35 pounds. Occurring singly and in schools, the dolphin feeds on invertebrates and a variety of fishes, including flyingfishes. Thirty-two species of fishes belonging to nineteen families have been taken from the stomachs of Atlantic dolphins.

The small pompano dolphin *(C. equisetis)* and the common dolphin *(C. hippurus)*—the only members of the family—are very similar and are often confused. They can usually be differentiated, however, by the number of rays in

Jack mackerel (Trachurus symmetricus) schooling; Pacific marine.

the dorsal fin; the common dolphin has 55 to 65 and the pompano dolphin 48 to 55. The adult pompano is a small fish, reaching maturity at 12 inches and having a maximum size of 30 inches.

One surprising fact about the dolphin concerns its edibility: in the Hawaiian Islands, mahimahi is a premium fish and is in great demand, while in the Philippines and along some tropical American coasts it is considered a third-rate food fish. The growth rate of the dolphin is exceptionally rapid, and the entire life span is quite short, possibly no longer than two or three years.

Snappers (Family Lutjanidae)

The carnivorous snappers have sharp jaw teeth and a "snapper look," which is due to the characteristically flattened top of the snout, giving the fish a shovel-headed appearance. In many tropical regions of the world the snappers are food fishes of major importance. The family includes about 250 species, of which some fifteen occur along the American Atlantic coasts. Fewer species are found along the Pacific coast, and none ranges as far north as southern California. Wherever snappers occur, they are usually present in large numbers. Many of the species reach lengths of 2 or 3 feet.

Although snappers are primarily marine in habitat, some species, such as the Atlantic gray snapper *(Lutjanus griseus)*, readily enter brackish and fresh waters. In the headwater springs of the Homosassa and other rivers along the west coast of Florida, snappers are usually a conspicuous component of the fish population.

For some snappers, shallow mangrove areas are important nursery grounds. Although most of them live at shallow or moderate depths, there are others, such as the silk snapper *(L. vivanus)*, which have a much deeper normal depth range (500 to 800 feet in the Bahama Banks).

Many of the snappers are quite beautiful, with shades of red and yellow predominating. The yellowtail snapper *(Ocyurus chrysurus)* is a 2-foot species widely distributed on both sides of the tropical Atlantic; it has yellow fins and a yellow line along the side of the body, and the upper portion is blue with yellow spots. Other distinctive American Atlantic species include the red- and yellow-striped lane snapper *(L. synagris)* and the yellow- and green-banded mutton-fish *(L. analis)*.

In the Pacific and the Caribbean, snappers have been responsible for the transmission of the tropical fish poisoning known as ciguatera. One of the larger

160   *Top: Vermilion snapper (Rhomboplites aurorubens); Atlantic marine.*
        Bottom: Bluelined snapper (Lutjanus viridis); Pacific marine.

American Atlantic species, the cubera snapper *(L. cyanopterus)*, 3.3 feet and 110 pounds, is suspected of being the carrier.

Tripletails *(Family Lobotidae)*

The small tripletail family has only two species: the black-banded *Datnoides quadrifasciatus* from the East Indies and the common tripletail *(Lobotes surinamensis)*, which may reach 40 inches and occurs in all tropical seas. The name "tripletail" comes from the appearance of the dorsal and anal fins which, together with the caudal fin, give the appearance of three tails. The body profile looks somewhat like that of the fresh-water sunfishes. Actually, the tripletails are most closely related to the sea basses.

The immature fishes, measuring 2 or 3 inches, camouflage themselves by turning sideways and floating at the surface like leaves. It is quite startling for someone who does not know the habits of the tripletail to see what looks like a dead leaf suddenly swim away.

Mojarras *(Family Gerreidae)*

The small, silvery, shallow-water mojarras are similar in many respects to the slipmouths of the Indo-Pacific; at times the two have been placed together in a single family. Like the slipmouths, the mojarras have a protractile mouth, but they have a different kind of sheathing along the base of the dorsal and anal fins; the mojarra sheath is formed by a small, scaled extension of the body, so that the fins can be more or less depressed into the resulting groove.

Some of the mojarras have wide ranges. For example, the 8-inch spotfin mojarra *(Eucinostomus argenteus)*, which is found from New Jersey to Rio de Janeiro, has an almost equally wide range on the Pacific coast of the Americas, coming as far north as California. In all, there are about fourty species; they form a tropical marine group extending to some degree into temperate waters. They move readily into brackish water, and some even go into fresh water.

Grunts *(Family Pomadasyidae)*

The grunts look much like the snappers, but they differ from them primarily in dentition. They have very weak jaw teeth instead of strong canines, but they do have potent pharyngeal teeth. They are found primarily in shallow-water, tropical marine habitats, often in great numbers. They generally feed at night. Some seventeen species are known from the Atlantic coast of the United States and two from the Pacific; most of the North American species are less than 15 inches in length, but a few reach 2 feet. Many are used as food fishes.

The grunts receive their name from the sounds they produce by grinding their sharp pharyngeal teeth together; the adjacent air bladder acts as a sounding box, amplifying the sounds. The sound the grunt makes is most audible when the fish is taken from the water, but it can also be heard underwater by means of a hydrophone or other acoustical device.

Young grunts of many species have lines along the sides of the body. With growth, these disappear in some species but are retained in others, such as the Atlantic smallmouth grunt, the tomtate, and the striped grunt. On the Pacific coast the salema is an attractively striped grunt, whereas the only other member of the family in that area, the 20-inch sargo *(Anisotremus davidsoni)*, is rather nondescript, with a single vertical bar on the side of the body.

Some grunts are known for their strange kissing activity. Whether this is courtship behavior or territorial aggressiveness has not been determined.

Porgies (Family Sparidae)

Members of the porgy family look somewhat like a cross between a blunt-headed snapper and a grunt. They are deep-bodied fishes, usually equipped with powerful canine or incisor teeth, and they may also have strong molar, or grinding, teeth. Most of the approximately 100 species in the family are found in tropical and temperate marine waters, but some have been able to adapt to very cold water and a few occasionally enter fresh water.

American porgies are generally less than 2 feet in length and occur at a maximum depth of 280 feet. There are fifteen porgies in the American Atlantic fauna. Typical of these species are the scup *(Stenotomus chrysops)*, the sheepshead or sea bream *(Archosargus rhomboidalis)*, and the pinfish *(Lagodon rhomboides)*. The first two are of some value as food and anglers' fishes.

There is only a single species, *Calamus brachysomus*, in the California fauna.

Croakers and Drums (Family Sciaenidae)

Noise production is a characteristic of most species of this family, provided the species has an air bladder. Muscles attached to the sides of the air bladder work

Overleaf: Barred grunt (Haemulon sexfasciatum); Pacific marine.

in the same way as the strings on a guitar, with the air bladder acting as a resonance chamber and amplifying the snapping of the muscles. A few of the sciaenids lack air bladders but sometimes produce a low-amplitude sound by grinding their teeth together. Among these are members of the genus *Menticirrhus*, including the California corbina *(M. undulatus)* and several Atlantic species such as the king whiting *(M. saxatilis)* and the gulf minkfish *(M. focaliger)*.

The croaker and drum family is of moderate size, numbering perhaps 160 species. The common names checklist shows 34 species of sciaenids in the United States and Canada, including ten from the Pacific coast. These are shallow-water, usually carnivorous fishes of tropical and temperate seas. Some species move readily into brackish and fresh water, and one, the American fresh-water drum *(Aplodinotus grunniens)*, ranging from Guatemala to Canada, does not return to saltwater. The croakers have two separate dorsal fins, which are usually barely connected at the base; a rounded snout is typical of many of them, and some have small barbels under the chin. The majority are marketable food fishes.

Aquarists consider the beautifully striped species of the tropical genus *Equetus*, including the high-hat, the jackknife-fish, and the cubbyu, to be the most spectacular members of this family. The first dorsal fin of these fishes is usually greatly elevated, and there are black and white bands over the entire body.

The Atlantic croaker *(Micropogon undulatus)*, which has a normal range of 1 to 4 pounds, is a well-known species throughout most of its habitat from Massachusetts to Argentina. The spot *(Leiostomus xanthurus)*, found from Cape Cod to Texas, is easily recognized by the spot above the base of the pectoral fin as well as by the fifteen or so oblique bars extending upward from the lateral line to the top of the back.

The red drum *(Sciaenops ocellata)*, sometimes called redfish or channel bass, is also easily recognized by the spot on the upper section of the caudal peduncle just ahead of the tail fin. Reaching a record weight of 83 pounds at a length of 52 inches, this valuable fish ranges from Massachusetts to Florida and the Gulf of Mexico.

The genus *Cynoscion* includes a number of croaker-like fishes, among them the California white seabass *(C. nobilis)* and the Atlantic weakfish or common sea trout *(C. regalis)*, as well as the various species of Atlantic squeteagues. The largest member of the family, the commercially important totuava *(C. macdonaldi)*, also belongs to this genus; it occurs in the Gulf of California and may weigh as much as 225 pounds.

It is of interest to note that several species of sciaenids have been introduced from the Gulf of California into California's inland Salton Sea, where they are now established and reproducing. One of these, the small gulf croaker *(Bairdiella icistia)*, forms the basis for the food cycle of the larger corvinas, which are popular sport and food fishes.

Goatfishes (Family Mullidae)

Two long, tactile barbels under the chin, constantly working like a mine detector as they are dragged over the bottom, enable the goatfishes to locate small items of food that might otherwise be missed. These barbels are highly flexible, often moving back and forth even when the goatfish is at rest. When not in use, the barbels can be pulled in under the throat, where they are fairly inconspicuous. The goatfish is elongate and has separate spiny-rayed and soft-rayed dorsal fins and a forked tail. Some have brilliant colors splashed with reds and yellows or with striped patterns.

About 55 species of goatfishes are recognized from the tropical and temperate marine waters of the world; the majority are less than 10 inches in length, but a few approach 2 feet. Typically, they are found inshore, often in shallow water. Some species are solitary; others travel in schools. They are carnivorous in diet, feeding principally on invertebrates.

The most common Atlantic species is probably the 11-inch spotted goatfish *(Pseudupeneus maculatus)*, which ranges from New Jersey to Brazil. Although capable of considerable color change, it can usually be identified by three blackish blotches on the upper part of the body. Another common species, the yellow goatfish *(Mulloidichthys martinicus)*, is found from Bermuda, Florida, and the Bahamas to Brazil. On the Pacific coast the Mexican goatfish *(P. dentatus)* ranges southward from southern California.

Sea Chubs (Family Kyphosidae)

This enlarged family includes the rudderfishes, nibblers, and halfmoons, all formerly recognized in separate families. The rudderfishes derive their name from the habit some species have of following behind ships, often for long distances. They are oval-shaped, schooling fishes with small mouths and fine teeth. There are fewer than a dozen species, most of them widely distributed. Several species are about 30 inches in length when full grown, but the majority are smaller.

Overleaf, top left: Pinfish (Lagodon rhomboides); Atlantic marine and fresh-water. Bottom left: Porkfish (Anisotremus virginicus); Atlantic marine. Right: Jackknife-fish (Equetus lanceolatus); Atlantic marine.

The Bermuda and yellow chub *(Kyphosus sectatrix* and *K. incisor)* are common species found on both sides of the Atlantic; both species are yellow-striped and primarily herbivorous.

While collecting fishes in 1971 in the Revillagigedo Islands (420 miles west of Colima, Mexico), I was amazed to find that a number of the normally dark rudderfishes *(K. lutescens)* had bright patches of yellow, or were completely yellow. One of these all-yellow fishes that was returned alive to Steinhart Aquarium in San Francisco later developed dark patches of pigment over most of the body. In this case the change may have been triggered by handling.

The nibblers are omnivorous marine fishes that have hinged lips and fine teeth that enable them to nibble very efficiently. Because of their irascible natures and constant pecking and nibbling at other fishes, and even at each other, they are disliked intensely by most aquarists. They are nondescript, oval-shaped fishes, greenish, gray, or black and usually less than 18 inches in length. Approximately a dozen species are known, most of them from the Pacific. The greenish opaleye *(Girella nigricans)* is an inshore California species, common from Monterey Bay to Baja California. One can easily identify this fish by the pair of conspicuous white spots on the back on each side of the dorsal fin.

Spadefishes (Family Ephippidae)

Some fifteen species of marine spadefishes are known from the tropical and temperate waters of the world. Two of these occur in North America: the Atlantic spadefish *(Chaetodipterus faber)* and its Pacific cousin, *C. zonatus.* The Atlantic species is the best known, ranging from Cape Cod to Brazil. It has been introduced into Bermudan waters and now appears to be well established there. It is noted for its liking for shellfish of all kinds. Sometimes during feeding it produces sounds, either by grinding its pharyngeal teeth together or by contracting muscles attached to an air bladder that may extend two thirds of the length of the fish.

Spadefishes are well known for their schooling activities. They are deep-bodied and laterally compressed with the spinous part of the dorsal fin quite distinct from the soft-rayed portion. In the young there are five or six conspicuous vertical bands extending around the body, but with growth these bands are lost. The young are quite dark, but they tend to become lighter until, at the maximum length of about 3 feet, the entire body is silvery.

Mexican goatfish (Pseudupeneus dentatus); Pacific marine.
Overleaf: Whitestripe angelfish (Holacanthus passer) schooling; Pacific marine.

Butterflyfishes and Angelfishes (Family Chaetodontidae)

In shallow, tropical waters around reefs, or in aquariums, the butterflyfishes and angelfishes always attract attention. Although usually solitary or in pairs, they sometimes travel in small groups, which makes their distinctive patterns even more striking. Their deep, laterally compressed bodies have characteristic markings that usually make each species easy to recognize. For example, the Atlantic spotfin, the foureye, and the banded butterflyfish have had their identifying marks incorporated into their common names. However, in maturing, some species undergo drastic pattern changes that complicate identification. The Atlantic French and gray angels *(Pomacanthus paru* and *P. arcuatus)* have brilliant semicircular yellow stripes when young, but lose them with growth. These pattern changes have been responsible for considerable confusion regarding names. Hybridization, which also occurs in this family, has added to the confusion.

There are two main groups in the family: the angelfishes, which have a strong spine on the base of the preopercle, and the butterflyfishes, which lack the spine. About 190 species are recognized; the common names checklist shows twelve species in tropical Atlantic U.S. waters and only two on the Pacific side. However, as one moves south into the Caribbean and tropical American region, more species occur.

The butterflyfishes and angelfishes have a small mouth with many small teeth, and often have an extended snout well adapted to picking out small invertebrates from cracks and crevices in rocks and coral. Although these fishes are primarily carnivorous, there are some omnivorous as well as herbivorous species. A few species even serve as cleaners for other fishes. In the Gulf of California, the cleaning activity of the blacknose butterfly *(Heniochus nigrirostris)* is often observed by divers. In this same area, the longnose or forceps butterfly *(Forcipiger longirostris)* makes its first American appearance at the tip of Baja California. This Indo-Pacific fish is noted for its pugnacious nature, especially among its own kind. The fighting is done with the dorsal fin spines, which stand erect as *Forcipiger* turns at an angle to bring them into contact with other fish. Because of this aggressiveness, these fish must be shipped individually or with other species.

The smallest angelfishes belong to the genus *Centropyge*. In parts of the American tropical Atlantic the 2.5-inch cherubfish *(C. argi)* is a very active reef fish. With its dark blue body and orange head it has become a favorite with aquarists, but is difficult to collect since its preferred habitat is more than 100 feet down.

Since the majority of easily observed chaetodonts were described by early ichthyologists more than 100 years ago, about the only place that one can now find a new species of butterflyfish or angelfish is in deep water. In 1958 Hubbs and Rechnitzer discovered the scythe butterfly *(Chaetodon falcifer)*, suspected of being a deep-water denizen and now known to range from southern California to the Galapagos Islands. At Cape San Lucas, Baja California, observations from the diving saucer of the famous marine explorer, Jacques Cousteau, revealed moderate numbers of this otherwise rare fish at a depth of about 325 feet.

Cichlids (Family Cichlidae)

The cichlids look much like the common North American centrarchid sunfishes familiar to most fresh-water fishermen, but the cichlids have a single nostril, whereas the centrarchids have a double nostril. A nasty disposition and an aggressive nature are recognized traits of most cichlids. More than 600 species are known, with the largest number found in the fresh waters of Africa and South America. Many of the species of cichlids on the two continents are similar, and since these fishes cannot survive in full-strength sea water, zoogeographers have used this evidence that the two continents were once united.

Since the cichlids are primarily a tropical, fresh-water family, the number of species decreases as one moves northward from the Amazon, until, in the United States, there is only a single native species, the Rio Grande perch *(Cichlasoma cyanoguttatum)* of southern Texas.

One of the largest genera is *Cichlasoma*, which in Mexico alone has some 44 species. The most spectacular in this genus is the red devil cichlid *(C. labiatum)* from the region of Lake Nicaragua. Because of variable color patterns, it was formerly known by several species names. Individuals with the characteristic brilliant orange-red color are popular among aquarists. Mature males develop a very large bump on the forehead. A speckled cichlid *(C. managuense)* from this same area has also found favor with the aquarists.

Since several species of African mouthbrooders of the large genus *Tilapia* have been introduced in the United States, it is of interest to examine their remarkable reproductive pattern. *Tilapia* reproduce rapidly, usually in fresh water, rarely in saltwater. Using its mouth, the male digs a small crater in sand or mud and entices a receptive female to lay her eggs in the depression. The

eggs are quickly fertilized; then the female, or, in a few species, the male, picks up the eggs and holds them in the mouth for as long as three weeks until they hatch. The time required for hatching is dependent upon the species and the temperature. Even after hatching, the young may be held in the mouth for a short time, after which they are carefully guarded for a few more days. If threatened, the youngsters swim back into the parent's mouth.

There are at least eight species of exotic cichlids now established in the United States, most of them in southern Florida. Some have been released from aquarium stocks, and aquarists will recognize such well-known names as the Central American convict cichlid *(Cichlasoma nigrofasciatum)*, the South American oscar *(Astronotus ocellatus)*, and the black acara *(Aequidens portalegrensis)*.

Other cichlids may have been introduced in this country because of their food value. For example, the African sunfish, or black mouthbrooder *(Tilapia melanotheron)*, has been marketed in Tampa, Florida, with some individual catches in nearby Bullfrog Creek as large as 1,553 pounds. Another African fish, the Mozambique mouthbrooder *(T. mossambica)*, has become established in Florida, Texas, Montana, and Hawaii. The first of these fishes brought into the United States from Africa were transshipped to Hawaii through Steinhart Aquarium in San Francisco. The Hawaiian Department of Fish and Game planned to study the species and its ability to remove vegetation from ditches and canals. Although the species did not serve the purpose, it is now established in some Hawaiian fresh waters; and there are reproducing marine populations as well. Some of the Steinhart progeny were sent to the San Antonio Aquarium, where they were—unfortunately, as it turned out—placed in a holding pen in a stream adjacent to the aquarium. Escapees from this enclosure eventually moved through two water systems where the Rio Grande perch *(Cichlasoma cyanoguttatum)* had previously been the sole member of the family. Whenever the two species came into contact, the more belligerent newcomer quickly took over the habitat. A fish introduction, whether planned or accidental, may have serious consequences and deserves careful handling.

Surfperches (Family Embiotocidae)

Twenty-three species of mostly marine fishes make up this remarkable family of surfperches. Two species occur in Japan and Korea, and other species are found from southern Alaska south to central Baja California. They range in size from the 18-inch rubberlip seaperch *(Rhacochilus toxotes)*, noted for its fleshy lips,

Top: Pacific spadefish (Chaetodipterus zonatus). Bottom: Pacific sea chub (Kyphosus lutescens); Both, Pacific marine. Rare photo of normal and yellow phases. Overleaf, left: Blacknose butterflyfish (Heniochus nigrirostris). Pacific marine. Right: Queen angelfish (Holacanthus ciliaris); Atlantic marine.

to species 6 inches or less in length. Of this group of small species the commonest is the shiner perch *(Cymatogaster aggregata)*. The common names of the embiotocids are derived from their preferred habitats; for example, six species live mostly in the surf and are recognized as surfperches, with individual names such as barred, calico, and silver. Three species live in the sea, but not in the surf, and are called seaperches. The remainder, with other habitats, such as tide pools, deep water, and fresh water, are simply called perches.

The embiotocids are different from the majority of other marine fishes in that the young are born alive, a discovery first made in 1853 at Sausalito and soon thereafter reported by Harvard's great zoologist, Louis Agassiz. Live birth requires impregnation of the female by the male, who uses the thickened forward end of the anal fin for this purpose. With the exception of the striped seaperch *(Embiotoca lateralis)*, surfperches become sexually mature very early, and the first act of copulation takes place soon after birth. The breeding season varies according to temperature. Along the California coast breeding usually takes place during the summer, but at the time of copulation the sperm does not touch the eggs, and fertilization does not take place until a later period, ranging from fall to the following spring. The eggs have little yolk, and the young receive their nourishment and respiration through the ovarian fluid that bathes them.

Some species of embiotocids may leave their usual habitat at spawning time and enter bays to drop their young. In San Francisco Bay the shiner seaperch is usually the predominant fish, not only in numbers but often in total body volume as well.

The pink seaperch *(Zalembius rosaceus)* is found only in an offshore deeper-water habitat; some species occur in tide pools, and the tule perch *(Hysterocarpus traski)* is found in California in the Sacramento River delta and in Clear Lake. One peculiarity of distribution is that two species, the southern California island seaperch *(Cymatogaster gracilis)* and the Guadalupe seaperch *(Micrometrus aletes)*, are entirely insular and do not reach the mainland, although it is only a short distance away. Some of the larger species are well known to both sport and commercial fishermen, the white seaperch *(Phanerodon furcatus)* being among the most important commercial species in the family.

Most of the species in the embiotocid family can be described as nondescript in color. By contrast the striped and rainbow seaperches *(Embiotoca lateralis* and *Hypsurus caryi)* are brightly colored, with blue stripes running the length of the body. The shiner perch *(C. aggregata)* normally has vertical yellow bars

Top: French angelfish (Pomacanthus paru), juvenile; Atlantic marine.
Bottom: Rio Grande perch (Cichlasoma cyanoguttatum); fresh-water.

on the sides of the body, but during breeding season the males develop black horizontal lines that largely obscure the yellow.

Damselfishes (Family Pomacentridae)

The damselfishes are laterally compressed, tropical to temperate marine fishes usually no larger than 6 inches. There are about 215 species, all characterized by single rather than double nostrils. They are worldwide in distribution, and fairly abundant in the areas where they occur. Colors range from drab to spectacular. Juveniles often have brilliant markings that may be radically different from the dull appearance of the adult. As a family group, they are noted for their belligerent dispositions, although some species are docile enough to be desirable aquarium fishes.

The common names checklist shows thirteen species along the Atlantic coast of the United States and in the Bahamas but only two species in California.

The common Atlantic threespot damselfish *(Eupomacentrus planifrons)* is a bright yellow, 5-inch species that is sometimes captured by tropical fish collectors. In spite of protective legislation collectors also take the most brightly colored denizen of the California kelp habitat, the garibaldi *(Hypsypops rubicunda)*. Spawning for this species takes place during July and August, and is initiated by the male's cleaning an area surrounding a lump of red algae; it is upon this plant that the female deposits her eggs. The blue-spotted juveniles, which are entirely different in color from the adults, appear between August and November. By the time they are about 2.5 inches in length they begin to acquire the color of the adults. In aquariums, the adults are noted for the highly audible clicking noises they make with their pharyngeal teeth, especially at feeding time. Like most damsels, the garibaldis are quarrelsome fishes with strong territorial patterns. In captivity, if they are overcrowded and not allowed places to hide, they quickly kill the weaker or smaller fish of their kind.

Although many of the damsels are typically inshore species, some, such as the American Atlantic blue chromis *(Chromis cyaneus)*, are generally found offshore. Damselfishes of the genus *Dascyllus* are often found around coral heads, several hundred of the same species hovering a foot or so above a large head; if danger threatens—perhaps in the form of a skin diver approaching—they move in unison back into the interstices of the coral.

The two largest genera of damselfishes are *Pomacentrus* and *Abudefduf;* the majority of these fishes do not have particularly brilliant markings. One of the

Preceding pages, left: Rainbow seaperch (Hypsurus caryi), painted greenling (Oxylebius pictus) among Telia anemones. Right, top to bottom: Black perch (Embiotoca jacksoni). Garibaldi (Hypsypops rubicunda); All, Pacific marine. Yellowtail damselfish (Microspathodon chrysurus); Atlantic marine.

most widely distributed fishes in the family is the sergeant major *(A. saxatilis)*, a vertically banded 4-inch fish that occurs on both sides of the Atlantic and in the Pacific. It has a most unpleasant disposition.

Hawkfishes (Family Cirrhitidae)

The hawkfishes, with some 35 species, are primarily a tropical, Indo-Pacific group; but there are two Atlantic species, one on the American and one on the European coast. They are usually found in shallow water and are noted for their habit of watchful sitting and hiding, moving only occasionally from one spot to another. They have two important identifying characteristics: the simple rays of the pectoral fins are thickened and slightly extended, and there is a fringe at the back of each nostril. The dorsal fin spines may have fringes at the tip.

The brightly colored red-spotted 3.5-inch hawkfish *(Amblycirrhitus pinos)* is a well-known resident of the Bahamas, Florida, and the Antilles. Its first cousin is a similarly colored hawkfish *(Cirrhitichthys oxycephalus)* which is reasonably abundant in the southern end of the Gulf of California, where it is often found sitting on small coral heads.

Wrasses (Family Labridae)

The wrasses are mostly inshore tropical marine fishes with a few species that are able to stand temperate waters. Although more than 600 species have been described, ichthyologists have recently found that a number of them had been given two different names because males and females are radically different in color. Sometimes color changes occurring with growth have also proved confusing. For example, the common bluehead *(Thalassoma bifasciatum)*, which occurs on both sides of the tropical Atlantic, has highly variable young as well as adult males that have either blue or yellow heads. The blueheads mate singly with yellowhead females, whereas the mating of yellowhead males and similar females is a group affair. It is thought that the bluehead males are sex-reversed females, a phenomenon that sometimes happens in this family. To compound the confusion, the wrasse blenny *(Hemiemblemaria simulus)* of Florida and the Bahamas, which often swims with the blueheads, has a coloration that mimics them. Most of the wrasses and some of the parrotfishes have swimming patterns that are characteristic and easily recognized: the pectoral fins do the swimming so the fish usually appears to flit about.

Overleaf, left: Blue chromis (Chromis cyaneus); Atlantic marine. Top right: Sergeant major (Abudefduf saxatilis) guarding eggs; Atlantic marine. Bottom right: Red-spotted hawkfish (Cirrhitichthys oxycephalus); Pacific marine.

In size the wrasses range from 3 inches to 10 feet, and many have brilliant colors. They are usually nonschooling fishes and are noted for their well-developed incisor or canine teeth, which in some instances protrude like a pair of forceps from the protrusile mouth. Many of them have a vile disposition and use these teeth to remove the fins and eyes from other fishes and even to mutilate members of their own species. Needless to say, in spite of their beautiful colors, many wrasses are not desirable aquarium fishes.

Most of the smaller species of wrasses sleep on their sides in the sand at night. It is rather disconcerting to the aquarist not familiar with this activity to find that during the daytime he may have a tank filled with fifty of the kelp-dwelling señoritas *(Oxyjulis californica)* but at night the tank appears empty.

The blunt-headed razorfishes make use of the sand habitat during both day and night. An approaching diver sees the razorfish dive into sand and then thrust through it almost as fast as through water; they are not easy to capture. The 8-inch pearly razorfish *(Hemipteronotus novacula)* occurs on both sides of the Atlantic and in the North American area from North Carolina to Brazil.

The reddish hogfishes of the genus *Bodianus* are conspicuous members of the tropical marine fauna on both North American coasts. The 9-inch spotfin hogfish *(B. pulchellus)*, found from Florida to South America, is popular in the tropical fish trade. The common hogfish *(Lachnolaimus maximus)*, identified by its greatly extended first three dorsal fin rays, ranges throughout the Caribbean north to the Carolinas; it reaches a length of almost 3 feet and is used as a food fish. The male has a dark line extending from the base of the dorsal fin down over the snout, and the females are usually orange-red with a black spot at the base of the soft dorsal fin. Like many of the wrasses, there is much variation in color patterns.

In the Pacific kelp beds ranging from Monterey to Baja California, the spectacular male sheephead *(Pimelometopon pulchrum)* is a very conspicuous fish; it has a black head, white chin, and red body. Maximum size for the male is 3 feet and 36 pounds. The much smaller female is dull red and also has a white chin. In this species sex reversal is a normal pattern, so all small fish are females and all large fish are males.

Parrotfishes (Family Scaridae)

The colorful parrotfishes are all similar in appearance, so if you can recognize one species, you will undoubtedly be able to recognize others. The presence of

Giant hawkfish (Cirrhitus rivulatus); Pacific marine. Overleaf, left: Stoplight parrotfish (Sparisoma viride); Atlantic marine. Top right: Rainbow and bluehead wrasse (young and adult) of Thalassoma lucasanum; Pacific marine. Bottom right: Spotfin hogfish (Bodianus pulchellus); Atlantic marine.

heavy, parrot-like plate teeth will usually confirm the identification. These fishes are responsible for the breakdown of tropical reefs around the world. Coral and other hard materials, algae, and sea grasses are gouged out and then ground up by the pharyngeal teeth. A reef study in Bermuda showed an estimated one ton of material per acre per year passing through fish digestive tracts, and most of this was the work of parrotfishes.

The swimming pattern of the parrots is like that of the wrasses, with the pectoral fins doing most of the work. Also like the wrasses, they have two reproductive patterns—group spawning and single-pair spawning. In the latter, the male of the pair usually has a pattern different from that of other males and is thought to be a sex-reversed female or, in ichthyological jargon, a super male. With growth, some species of parrotfishes go through at least three entirely different color phases. In addition, the males and females are often totally different in coloration, causing great confusion in their scientific names. A few years ago approximately 350 species were recognized; this figure has now been reduced to about 80 as a result of careful field observations by diving biologists.

Some parrotfishes have set patterns of travel and go to certain areas regularly to defecate, leaving mounds of broken but undigested coral rubble that give mute testimony to their destructive effect. Parrots are often creatures of habit and demonstrate a strong homing instinct. For example, at Bermuda, the rainbow parrotfish *(Scarus guacamaia)* is a cave dweller and moves out during the day to forage. When frightened, it swims directly back to the cave; if a net is stretched across the entrance to the cave, it will repeatedly swim into the net in its efforts to return to its home.

Some parrotfishes, particularly of the genus *Scarus*, often sleep at night enveloped in a mucous cocoon. It may take the parrotfish thirty minutes or so to secrete this envelope and usually the same amount of time to break out of it. Emergence from the cocoon is triggered by the return of either natural or artificial light. The Atlantic bluelip parrotfish *(Cryptotomus roseus)*, 4.5-inches long, behaves more like a wrasse than a parrotfish and secretes its cocoon while sleeping hidden in the sand. It is one of the smallest in the family, being sexually mature at 2.5 inches.

The giants of the parrotfish family are found in the tropical Indo-Pacific where some species reach an average maximum length of 6 feet with giant bulls reported to reach 12 feet. There are fourteen species of parrotfishes in Florida and the Bahamas but none on the Pacific coast north of the Gulf of California, where seven have been recorded.

Male California sheephead (Pimelometopon pulchrum); Pacific marine.

Mullets (Family Mugilidae)

The mullets are torpedo-shaped, shallow-water, schooling fishes usually found over sandy or muddy bottom containing detritus, through which they normally grub for food. Most of the 100 or so species have a muscular, gizzard-like stomach which enables them to grind their food, primarily vegetable, before it starts through their exceptionally long digestive tract. A 13-inch mullet with a digestive tract 7 feet long is not unusual. The structure and curvature of the mouth and the arrangement of the teeth are important factors in determining the various genera. Mullets resemble the silversides in many respects: they have separate spiny-rayed and soft-rayed dorsal fins, the pelvic fins are abdominal in position, and the lateral line is vestigial or absent. But, unlike the silversides, the mullets do not have the silver band along the side of the body, and they usually have fewer vertebrae.

The majority of these worldwide fishes are tropical and temperate marine species, but they move readily into brackish and fresh water. In both the East Indies and the West Indies some species of mullets are normally restricted to fresh water.

The most widely distributed mullet species in the Atlantic and Pacific is the striped mullet *(Mugil cephalus)*, which may reach a length of 3 feet and a weight of 15 pounds.

Barracudas (Family Sphyraenidae)

Divers are sometimes more fearful of attack by giant carnivorous barracudas than by sharks. Barracudas are inquisitive, and although they do not exactly stalk a diver, they follow him around. Since they apparently feed by sight rather than by smell, they may sample any object that is brightly colored or that makes erratic movements, such as a wounded fish. Unlike a shark, a barracuda makes a single attack and leaves a clean wound with no jagged edges. The jutting lower jaw and fanglike teeth of these elongated, torpedo-shaped fishes are so well known that barracudas require little identification. The two dorsal fins are separated by a wide distance. Although they resemble the fresh-water pikes, barracudas are, of course, marine fishes; they are usually found in tropical waters, but some species range into temperate seas. Despite the fact that they have occasionally been involved in cases of tropical-fish poisoning, all of the twenty species are usually considered excellent and tasty food fishes. A 1970

Great barracuda (Sphyraena barracuda); Atlantic marine.

report on the incidence of ciguatera in nineteen specimens of *Sphryaena barracuda* from the west coast of Florida showed a low virulence in the viscera of three individuals, but the flesh was not toxic.

Six feet is the normal maximum length of the several species of large barracudas, but there are unverified reports of some growing to twice that length. The American Fisheries Society list of common names shows four American Atlantic species and one Pacific species.

Threadfins (Family Polynemidae)

Typical of the threadfins, sometimes called tasselfishes, is an anchovy-type head with rounded nose and recessed lower jaw; the mouth, which is on the underside of the head, is not obvious unless it is open. There are two dorsal fins, widely separated, and a deeply forked tail fin. The threadfin takes its name from the

195

Jawfish (Opistognathus rhomaleus) brooding eggs in mouth; Pacific marine.

peculiar division of the pectoral fin into an upper section with the rays attached to each other, as in a normal fin, and an entirely separate ventral section composed of four to seven individual long filamentous rays. These slender rays are under voluntary control and are thought to have a tactile function; they are usually carried close against the body so that they are not visible, but the fish can quickly swing them outward—and often does—so that many slender fingers extend like the tines of a rake beneath the fish.

The threadfins, which are found throughout most of the world's tropics, usually favor an inshore marine habitat and are often found in great abundance in estuaries and river mouths. Most of the three dozen or so species are full grown at a length of less than 18 inches, but at least one, the Indo-Pacific *Eleutheronema tetradactylum*, reaches a length of 6 feet. They are highly prized as food fishes. The Atlantic and littlescale threadfins and the barbu are the most common Atlantic species, whereas the blue and yellow bobos are the Pacific representatives.

Sandfishes (Family Trichodontidae)

The sandfishes are scaleless northern Pacific marine species. They have nearly vertical mouths with peculiar fringed lips that provide instant identification. Another identifying detail is the preopercle, which has five sharp spines. The sandfish's normal position is on the bottom, buried in the mud or sand, with only its mouth and eyes showing. Two species are known, both with a maximum size of about 12 inches: the first, *Trichodon trichodon*, ranges from northern

Yellowhead jawfish (Opistognathus aurifrons); Atlantic marine.   197

California to Alaska and can be identified by its fourteen or fifteen dorsal fin spines; the second, *Arctoscopus japonicus*, is found from Alaska to Korea and has ten or eleven dorsal fin spines. Since the latter is an important food fish in parts of Japan, its biology is well known. During most of the year it is found at depths of around 450 feet, but during December it moves into water less than 3 feet deep to spawn. An average of about 750 eggs are laid in spherical capsules. Hatching requires up to two months, after which the juveniles remain in shallow water for three months before moving into deeper water.

Jawfishes (Family Opistognathidae)

The advent of Self Contained Underwater Breathing Apparatus made possible the discovery by diving biologists of the fascinating habits of the tropical marine jawfishes. The diver looks for holes in the sand, each surrounded by telltale small rocks and coral which the jawfish has carefully selected. The blunt head of the jawfish will often appear at the entrance of the hole, cautiously watching the diver. These fishes have a remarkable ability to dig holes in sand and gravel, spitting each mouthful outside the hole. Carrying sand and rock by mouth is such a constant activity that even if the jawfish is mouth-brooding eggs, it will periodically spit out the eggs in order to do some housecleaning in the burrow. Following this, the eggs are carefully picked up. The jawfish family is a small one, with probably no more than 26 species. Of these, some thirteen are in the western Atlantic; about eight are on the North American Pacific coast in and south of the Gulf of California.

Most jawfishes sit at the entrance of the burrow but will occasionally dart out for food or for territorial defense. Returning to the hole is usually accomplished by swimming backward, entering tail first. A notable exception is an undescribed species in the Gulf of California that hovers above the hole with its blackish dorsal and anal fins widely expanded. After a few seconds of this startling display, the "black-flag" jawfish darts into its hole, not tail first, but head first. In the same area other jawfish without the "black flag" enter tail-first. The difference in entry may be a male-female characteristic.

Hovering above the hole is not characteristic of most of the carnivorous jawfishes. However, the 4-inch yellowhead jawfish *(Opistognathus aurifrons)*, found from Florida to the West Indies, spends much of its time snapping up zooplankton above the hole. This hovering activity has made it very popular with marine aquarists. The male incubates the eggs in the mouth.

At different times at Steinhart Aquarium we have observed two giant jaw-fishes *(O. rhomaleus)*, found in the Gulf of California, which have carried eggs in the mouth. The first jawfish had five consecutive clutches, and the second had four. Each clutch was carried for 3.5 to 4 days, during which time the parent would often revolve the egg mass in the mouth. The time between spawnings varied from ten to thirty days. Although we tried several techniques, we were not successful in hatching the eggs. Sectioning of the gonads revealed that the mouth-brooding fishes were females.

Ronquils (Family Bathymasteridae)

The ronquils are small, elongate bottom-dwelling fishes found at moderate depths in the North Pacific. About seven species are recognized, and some have attractive color patterns. Maximum size is 12 inches or less. The biology of the species in this interesting family is unknown.

Sand Stargazers (Family Dactyloscopidae)

The species in this family, between twenty and twenty-five in number, are usually shallow-water dwellers and are often found buried in sand. They are limited to the New World and are mostly tropical marine species, although several enter estuaries and one American Pacific species sometimes enters fresh water. Some species carry the eggs in two spherical masses, one under each pectoral fin. In only one species has the sex of the egg carrier been determined—it is the male. The sand stargazers are almost identical to the uranoscopids, or electric stargazers, except that they lack the electrical organs and have one spine and three rays in each ventral fin; the uranoscopids have five rays in each fin.

The common sand stargazer *(Dactyloscopus tridigitatus)* is a small 3-inch species that ranges from Bermuda and the Gulf of Mexico to Brazil. Its very small eyes on long stalks provide easy identification. Our tropical Atlantic fauna includes several 2- to 3-inch members of the genus *Gillellus*; unlike most other stargazers, these fishes have the dorsal fin divided into three portions.

Electric Stargazers (Family Uranoscopidae)

A charge of fifty volts has been recorded from the electric organs of an ura-noscopid stargazer. These organs are located in a special pouch behind the eyes and are formed from modified eye tissue. The stargazers reverse the polarity found in the electric rays, and are negative on the upper surface and positive on the lower surface. Additional protective equipment includes two large poison spines just above the pectoral fins and behind the opercle. Each spine has double grooves along the sides and a venom gland at the base. Venom from these spines has been known to be responsible for the death of humans. The ventral or pelvic fins are located under the throat, and the mouth, with its fringed lips, is in nearly vertical position. Some stargazers have small wormlike fishing lures attached to the mouth, which are used to entice passing food fishes as the stargazer lies buried in the sand. When seen in this position, it is obvious why the fish has been named "stargazer," for the eyes are on top of the head and look directly upward. Some stargazers have nostrils that open into the mouth, enabling the buried fish to bring water into the gill cavity with less sediment than if the mouth were used for this purpose, as is normal in other fishes. The uranoscopid stargazers form a small family whose members range from shallow to very deep tropical and temperate marine waters around the world. The 12-inch northern stargazer *(Astroscopus guttatus)* has a limited range from New York to Virginia. In warmer waters its counterpart is the 15-inch southern stargazer *(A. y-graecum)*.

Clinids (Family Clinidae)

The clinids form a large family, mostly of small fishes found in subtropical and temperate seas, predominantly in the Southern Hemisphere. Some 180 species are recognized. A number are exotically marked and colored and have fascinating life histories. Most of them bear their young alive, and the males have a large intromittent organ.

The 8-inch hairy blenny *(Labrisomus nuchipinnis)*, found on both sides of the tropical Atlantic, is a typical representative of the important genus *Labrisomus*, which occurs in both the Atlantic and the Pacific. It has the blunt-headed profile characteristic of many of the clinids. On the other hand, the beautiful brown and white mottled 2-foot kelpfish *(Heterostichus rostratus)*, the largest member of the family, is a representative of the point-headed group of scaled blennies; it is found from British Columbia to Baja California and is noted for its ability to match the color of its background. The males of the Florida bluethroat pikeblenny *(Chaenopsis ocellata)* are known for aggressiveness in maintaining their territories. If one male invades the territory of another, he is instantly met

Top: Smooth ronquil (Rathbunella hypoplecta); Pacific marine.
Bottom: Flagtail sculpin (Aponema species); Pacific marine.

with the usual combat position: opened mouth and erected dorsal fin. The record for one of the largest mouths in proportion to the size of the fish undoubtedly goes to the male sarcastic fringehead *(Neoclinus blanchardi)*, a 9-inch American Pacific species with an extremely elongated jaw that allows the mouth to open like a vast scoop shovel.

Combtooth Blennies (Family Blenniidae)

These scaleless tropical and temperate blennies are divided into two groups according to the way the teeth are anchored. If the jaw teeth are fixed and immovable, the fish belongs in the subfamily Blenniinae; but if they are attached to the gums and can be moved, the fish is a member of the Salariinae. Many of the scaleless blennies, especially those of the subfamily Salariinae, go through a pelagic post-larval stage known as an ophioblennius. Crests, ridges, and fringes on the head are often helpful identification marks of many of the combtooth blennies. Members of *Blennius* and *Hypsoblennius* are well endowed in this respect. About 300 species of blennies are recognized; they are distributed throughout shallow tropical seas, and to a lesser extent in temperate waters. Common Atlantic species include the redlip blenny *(Ophioblennius atlanticus)* and the molly miller *(Blennius cristatus)*. Three common members of the genus *Hypsoblennius* occur on the Pacific coast: the bay, the rockpool, and the mussel blennies.

Pricklebacks (Family Stichaeidae)

The 54 kinds of pricklebacks usually have moderately elongated bodies covered with overlapping scales. The rays of the dorsal fin are entirely spiny in most species, but in a few there may be some soft rays at the end of the fin. Several species lack the pelvic fins. The pricklebacks are Northern Hemisphere, usually cold-water, marine fishes living in shallow water; there is one species, however, the Alaskan longsnout prickleback *(Lumpenella longirostris)*, which occurs as deep as 1,600 feet.

The 16-inch decorated warbonnet *(Chirolophis polyactocephalus)*, ranging from Puget Sound to Alaska, is one of the most spectacular of the stichaeids: it has numerous cirri or whiskers on the top of the head, which make it look like a Christmas tree. The 20-inch rock prickleback *(Xiphister mucosus)* is a common intertidal fish from southern California to Alaska; it can be identified by the presence of two broad bands in the form of a V extending backward from each eye.

Gunnels (Family Pholidae)

"Eel-like blennies" would be an apt description of the very elongated gunnels, which are shallow-water marine species of the North Pacific and North Atlantic. The dorsal fin is composed entirely of spines, and there is an incomplete lateral line. Gunnels tend to hide under rocks and in crevices, so they are not easily observed. At low tide they are often left exposed, but are able to survive when surrounded by moist seaweed. Some of the dozen or so species have bright colors with a pattern of lines across the head and through the eye. The rock gunnel *(Pholis gunnellus)* is a common 6- to 12-inch inshore species found on both sides of the North Atlantic. It has about ten spots along the base of the long dorsal fin. Common Pacific coast species include the rockweed gunnel *(Xererpes fucorum)* and the saddleback gunnel *(Pholis ornata)*.

Wolffishes and Wolfeel (Family Anarhichadidae)

The giants of the blenny world are found in the wolffish family, with two of the species reaching lengths of 6.5 to 9 feet. The nine species of the family are cold-water marine fishes of the Northern Hemisphere, and five of these occur in American waters. They lack pelvic fins, and in addition to the obvious canine teeth in the front of the jaws they have massive grinding teeth in the back of the mouth. There are two types: the wolffishes, which have a shorter body with about 85 vertebrae and a small tail fin; and the American Pacific wolfeel, which has a longer body with about 350 vertebrae and a pointed tail.

The 5-foot Atlantic wolffish *(Anarhichas lupus)* and the 6.5-foot spotted wolffish *(A. minor)* are both fished commercially along the European coasts, but only the former is commercially important in American waters.

Spawning of wolfeels *(Anarrhichthys ocellatus)*, a rare event, has been recorded at the Tacoma Aquarium in Tacoma, Washington, by Cecil Brousseau.

Dragonets (Family Callionymidae)

"Scooter blenny" is the term given to the dragonets by the Pacific import fish jobbers, and although these fishes are not blennies, they certainly do appear

Overleaf, top left: Molly miller (Blennius cristatus); Atlantic marine.
Bottom left: Signal blenny (Emblemaria hypacanthus); Pacific marine.
Right: Penpoint gunnels (Apodichthys flavidus); Pacific marine.

to scoot over the bottom as though they were riding on a cushion of air. These shallow-water, bottom-dwelling marine fishes occur in the tropics around the world. The adult size range for the approximately forty species in the family is 4 to 8 inches. Three species are known from the western Atlantic, of which the lancer dragonet *(Callionymus bairdi)* is the most common.

Dragonets can often be identified by the sharp spine on the gill cover, usually in the form of a hook, and by the very small gill opening at the top of the flattened head. The male dragonets usually have a much longer first dorsal fin than the females, and often flick the fin up and down in rapid succession. Whether this is territorial defense or courtship display is not known.

GOBIES AND THEIR RELATIVES *(Suborder Gobioidei)*

More than 700 species of goby-like fishes are known, which makes them the largest group of primarily marine fishes. Many survive easily in brackish water and some spend all of their lives in fresh water. Generally speaking, they are shallow-water fishes of the tropics, with fewer species occurring northward in temperate areas. For example, there are fifteen species of gobies in California, with the concentration greatest in the southern area and decreasing progressively northward. Chesapeake Bay has three species, but in the warm waters of the Bahamas there are 43. Bright colors are characteristic of some species. The majority of gobies are less than 6 inches in length, although a few may reach 1 or 2 feet. In North America only two of the five recognized gobioid families are represented.

Gobies and Sleepers *(Family Gobiidae)*

The typical goby has two dorsal fins and is between 2 and 4 inches in length. It spends much of its time sitting on the bottom or hiding in cracks, crevices, sponges, dead shells, or almost any variety of inshore habitat available. Some gobies have highly specialized ecological niches, and a few have become effective cleaners, removing parasites and detritus from other species. Most of the gobies are equipped with a cuplike sucker under the forward part of the body, formed by a partial or complete uniting of the two inner edges of the pelvic fins. By contrast, the sleeper-type gobies or eleotrids usually have the pelvic fins close together but not united.

Holes in a sand or silt bottom are the preferred shelter for many gobies. For

Pacific wolfeel (Anarrhichthys ocellatus); Pacific marine.

example, the 4-inch Caribbean hovering goby *(Ioglossus helenae)* is a zooplankton feeder, but with the approach of danger it dives into its home, a U-shaped burrow in the sand. The pink 2.5-inch southern California blind goby *(Typhlogobius californiensis)* lives its entire life in holes that have been dug by the ghost shrimp, *Callianassa*. Usually each hole contains a pair of shrimps, and sometimes a pair of gobies as well. The current pumped through the burrow by the shrimps brings food, some of which is utilized by the gobies. If the shrimps die, the gobies will not survive unless they find another host.

A miniature population explosion has hit the central California area in the form of the 9.5-inch Japanese goby *(Acanthogobius flavimanus)*, which first appeared in the Sacramento delta in 1963, has since spread over the entire San Francisco Bay, and is now moving outward. A highly competitive species, it appears to be moving into the habitat of several native gobies.

The small gobies of the genus *Lythrypnus* are noted for their distinctive banded patterns. The minute island goby *(L. nesiotes)*, found from the Bahamas to Venezuela, has a rich brown and white banded pattern, whereas the related spotwing goby *(L. spilus)*, found from the Bahamas to Haiti, has a large black

Sharknose goby (Gobiosoma evelynae); Atlantic marine.

Blue-banded goby (Lythrypnus dalli); Pacific marine.

spot at the base of the pectoral fin. The spectacular Pacific members of the
genus include the brilliant orange-red zebra goby *(Lythrypnus zebra)* and the
similarly colored blue-banded goby *(L. dalli)*. The latter species was originally
described in 1890 from specimens found at Catalina Island, and was considered
rare for many years. With the advent of scuba, divers discovered that this was
one of the more common inshore fishes of California. Today it is almost as
popular with the aquarist as the 2-inch neon goby *(Gobiosoma oceanops)*, one
of Florida's best cleaner fishes. The reproductive pattern of the neon is typical
of many gobies. They usually spawn twice a year—in spring and fall. The
parents select a clean surface, such as the inside of a shell, on which to deposit
about 100 eggs. During the incubation period of usually less than two weeks,
the eggs are carefully guarded by the parents. After hatching, the young remain
with the parents for several weeks. One year is required to reach adult size.

The frillfin goby *(Bathygobius soporator)* is an ugly fish, but it is certainly
the most studied of the American Atlantic gobies. This is partly due to its

abundance and wide distribution on both sides of the Atlantic; on the American side it ranges from North Carolina to Brazil. The frillfin's reproductive behavior is also noteworthy. After the male has prepared the nest, the female lays 15,000 to 18,000 eggs during a strenuous three- to nine-hour period. She then leaves, and the male takes over the guarding of the eggs until hatching occurs some five to seven days later. Egg-laying may be repeated in seven to sixteen days. The frillfin is easily identified by the upper five pectoral rays which are free and not connected by a membrane. Other gobies do not have this frillfin.

The word "sleeper" well describes the lethargic goby-like fishes of the genera *Dormitator, Eleotris, Gobiomorus,* and others. These fishes lack the sucker cup formed by the pelvic fin typical of most gobies, and they are larger, some reaching 1 to 2 feet. Previously, they were recognized as a separate family, the Eleotridae. They seem to prefer brackish and fresh water more than the other gobies. The fat sleeper *(Dormitator maculatus),* found from North Carolina to Brazil, is one of the common species.

Wormfishes (Family Microdesmidae)

These are secretive small fishes with a single many-rayed dorsal fin. Although they are goby relatives, one would never realize this from their appearance. All 25 known species are inhabitants of shallow tropical marine waters; six are found in North American Atlantic regions and twelve in the eastern Pacific. The 3-inch pugjaw wormfish *(Microdesmus floridanus)* is occasionally found in the Florida Keys and in the Bahamas.

Surgeonfishes (Family Acanthuridae)

Just in front of the tail, on the sides of the caudal peduncle, the surgeonfishes have the sharp "knives" which not only are the source of their name, but also are a mark of identification. The members of the genus *Acanthurus* have jack-knife-type structures that are hinged so that the "blade" drops into a hidden groove. The hinge is at the posterior end of the blade and the opened blade faces forward. Other surgeons, such as members of the genera *Naso* and *Prionurus,* have one to several spines in approximately the same position on the tail as those of *Acanthurus,* but the spines are immovable. The Indo-Pacific unicorn fishes are typical of this group. All of these knives are very sharp and capable of inflicting a serious cut on the hand of a careless fisherman.

The herbivorous surgeonfishes comprise a tropical marine group of about 75 species, most of which are less than 20 inches in length. Some of them are important food fishes. There are a few species, however, such as the Indo-Pacific convict fish *(A. triostegus)*, that have been involved in cases of tropical-fish poisoning. A major portion of the normal surgeon diet is composed of algae, which the fishes obtain by scraping rocks and coral. This makes it difficult for some species to be maintained in captivity.

The common American Atlantic ocean surgeon *(A. bahianus)* is one of the species that has been observed to make use of other fishes to remove ectoparasites and other detritus from its body. It is probable that other surgeons would make use of this service if the proper cleaner fish or invertebrate were present.

All surgeons go through a transparent larval stage known as acronurus, and this is sometimes followed by drastic growth and color changes. For example, the Atlantic blue tang *(A. coeruleus)* has a deceptively different-looking juvenile phase that is bright yellow in color.

Moorish Idol (Family Zanclidae)

Because of its beauty, the spectacular 7-inch moorish idol *(Zanclus canescens)* is usually selected by artists as the typical fish of the tropical Indo-Pacific reefs. On the Pacific American coast it ranges from Cape San Lucas at the tip of Baja California southward into tropical waters.

Young moorish idols have a sharp spine at each corner of the mouth; as the fish grows, these spines are lost and protuberances develop in front of the eyes. In the aquarium it is difficult to keep moorish idols in a healthy condition. They fight with other fishes, go into shock easily, and are highly susceptible to a variety of diseases that are not especially troublesome to other tropical marine species.

Snake Mackerels (Family Gempylidae)

The fast-moving, carnivorous gempylids are found in the tropical and temperate marine waters of the world, usually in the depths, although there are some species that commonly occur near the surface. Gempylids, interchangeably called snake mackerels or escolars, have jutting lower jaws with wicked-looking vomerine teeth located in the front part of the roof of the mouth. Although snake mackerels resemble the more slender of the tuna-like fishes, they lack the lateral

tail ridge of those forms. Fewer than two dozen species and some ten genera are recognized. Most of these have oily flesh; thus they are not desirable as food fishes, even though some are eaten. One of the most widely distributed species is the 6-foot oilfish *(Ruvettus pretiosus)*, which is found around the world, usually at depths of about 2,400 feet.

Cutlassfishes (Family Trichiuridae)

Fewer than twenty species of oceanic, often deep-water fishes make up this intriguing family. A barracuda-like head armed with impressive dentition and a very slender, laterally compressed body are identifying characteristics of these fishes. The body tapers gradually either to a very small V-shaped tail or to a point. The dorsal fin begins just behind the head and extends almost the full length of the body; there is a small anal fin. One of the most widely distributed forms is the 5-foot Atlantic cutlassfish *(Trichiurus lepturus)*, which occurs not only in the Atlantic but also in the Indian and western Pacific oceans. In the Japanese area it is known to migrate into relatively shallow water in August and September to spawn. In many areas it is a moderately valuable food fish.

Along the western American coast the Pacific cutlassfish *(T. nitens)* is occasionally washed ashore. Such an event is often recorded in newspapers, and the nearest museum is invariably besieged with inquiries about the "weird-looking fish from the depths."

Tunas and Mackerels (Family Scombridae)

A typical mackerel or tuna has a very sleek, cigar-shaped, streamlined body followed by a narrow caudal peduncle and a large, strong tail sharply divided into individual lobes. The second dorsal and the anal fin are followed by a series of small finlets. In some species scalation is limited to a small area called a corselet, under the pectoral fins. Small keels are conspicuously present on the end of the caudal peduncle just in front of the tail fin. These are usually three in number, with the center one considerably larger than the other two. The mackerels lack the center keel but have the two small lateral ones.

Scombroid fishes range around the world in tropical, temperate, and even cold seas. Whether they are present at the surface or in the depths is sometimes determined by the water temperature as well as by the composition of the pelagic community. Although some species of tuna are distinctive and can easily be

Top: Yellowtail surgeon (Prionurus punctatus); Pacific marine.   213
Bottom: Blue tang (Acanthurus coeruleus); Atlantic marine.

recognized at a glance, there are others in which identification may depend on counts of the number of gill rakers, fin rays, and finlets, as well as internal examination to determine the striations and shape of the liver and the presence or absence of the air bladder. About forty species of scombroids are recognized.

The great bluefin *(Thunnus thynnus)* is the picturesque "titan of tunas," reaching a length of 14 feet and a weight of 1,800 pounds. The tremendous battle put up by the hooked bluefin makes it a great favorite of sport anglers, and it has been the subject of many books and articles by sports writers. The migration pattern of the Atlantic bluefin involves considerable movement along coastal areas, including perhaps the entire North Atlantic.

Several species of bluefin have been described from other parts of the world, including Australia, Japan, and California; some of these are probably separate populations of a single worldwide species, but others may be distinct. Another bluefin tuna, the albacore *(Thunnus alalunga)*, is one of the most easily recognized scombrids; its chief identifying feature is its very long pectoral or shoulder fin, which reaches backward beyond the second dorsal and anal fins. The white meat of the albacore makes it a premium tuna for market and canning purposes; consequently it is fished extensively in the offshore waters of the Pacific and to a lesser extent in the Atlantic. Although 80-pound albacores have been recorded, most of those caught weigh less than 40 pounds. Females are mature when they are six years old; at that time they weigh about 33 pounds. Capture of tagged Pacific albacore indicates that these fast swimmers may move across the entire Pacific. On the basis of tagging evidence as well as other data, the North Pacific population is considered a continuous and homogeneous one, with the mature fishes moving from temperate waters southward for spawning. The South Pacific population is thought to follow the same pattern in reverse. The Atlantic population of albacore has not been studied in as much detail.

The yellowfin tunas include several species, some of which are widely distributed around the world, usually in warmer waters than those frequented by the bluefin. The most common species of yellowfins in the Indo-Pacific is *Thunnus albacares*, which at maximum size may be 8 feet long and weigh 450 pounds. It has been known to gain as much as 60 pounds in a single year. Studies have shown that there are several distinct yellowfin populations in the Pacific and that these populations do not tend to mix. Because of the tremendous abundance of these fishes, they are used to a considerable extent for canning purposes. The yellowfin in the Atlantic are not nearly as abundant as those in the Pacific, although they are considered the same species.

Top: Moorish idols (Zanclus canescens); Pacific marine.
Bottom: Skipjack tuna (Euthynnus pelamis); Atlantic-Pacific marine.

The widely distributed bigeye tuna *(T. obesus)* looks a great deal like the common yellowfin but apparently spends most of its time in deeper water. The eye is slightly larger than that of the yellowfin, the pectoral fin is longer, and there are striations on the edges of the liver—all features that are not easily recognized and have caused much confusion in the identification of the bigeye.

There are several species of small spotted tuna; these have dark meat and are not considered as desirable as the white meat types. The spots, varying in number from one to nine or ten, are located under the pectoral fin. The black skipjack *(Euthynnus lineatus)* is the common Pacific species, and the little tunny *(E. alletteratus)* is a similar Atlantic species.

Economically, the most important striped tuna is the skipjack *(E. pelamis)*, a fish that occurs in all tropical seas; it has a maximum weight of about 50 pounds at a length of 40 inches. This fast-moving tuna supports important local fisheries in many parts of the world. The stripes on the skipjack occur on the abdomen.

The bonitos have stripes on the upper part of the body. The Atlantic bonito *(Sarda sarda)* is found on both sides of the Atlantic and has a wide latitudinal range; in the western Atlantic it ranges from Nova Scotia to Argentina, and along the American Pacific coasts *S. chiliensis* occurs from California to Chile. Bonitos are predominantly white-meat species and consequently are often used for canning.

Heading the list of economically important mackerel is the Atlantic species *Scomber scombrus*, which looks like a small tuna. It reaches a maximum length of only 22 inches and a weight of 4 pounds. The movements of the Atlantic mackerel are well known: it appears each year around April in American waters off Chesapeake Bay and by June and July has moved into the waters off Maine; later, usually in September, the reverse migration begins. The chub mackerel *(S. japonicus)*, abundantly present in temperate marine waters on both American coasts as well as in the western Pacific, is also an important commercial species.

The Spanish mackerels, genus *Scomberomorus*, are very elongated, tuna-like fishes with a worldwide distribution. The American Atlantic *S. cavalla*, sometimes called the kingfish or king mackerel, which attains a weight of 100 pounds and a length of slightly more than 5 feet, is probably the largest species. The cero *(Scomberomorus regalis)* is another large species, and it ranges from New England to Brazil. Both it and the common Spanish mackerel *(S. maculatus)* are spotted. In Pacific tropical waters the sierra *(S. sierra)* is a favorite of the sport fisherman. These fishes are excellent food, and important fisheries exist for them in many areas.

California scorpionfish (Scorpaena guttata); Pacific marine.

Related to the Spanish mackerel is the wahoo *(Acanthocybium solanderi)*, another fast-moving, very elongated tuna-type. It is found around the world in tropical marine waters and at its maximum weight will tip the scale at more than 120 pounds. I have examined many of these fish, and the end of the stomach of each has invariably contained a single large, pink leechlike fluke, *Hirundinella ventricosa*. Some species of tuna also have these stomach flukes. As yet no one has solved the mystery of how these parasites get into the stomach.

The frigate or bullet mackerels are the least glamorous of all the tuna-like fishes. The meat is dark, and in many regions they are considered third-rate fish. Due to their abundance, however, they do form an important protein resource. *Auxis thazard,* found in tropical marine waters around the world, is the most common species.

At this point a comment on the future food supply for the world's expanding human population may be warranted. Our greatest untapped protein resource is to be found in the upper depths of the ocean, specifically in the schools of tuna and similar fast-moving fishes that are at present caught only accidentally on long-line fishing gear. Development of future fishing techniques, perhaps using deep-fishing submarines, will enable the world to make use of this vast protein reservoir.

Sailfishes, Spearfishes, and Marlins (Family Istiophoridae)

This family includes some of the world's most popular marine sport fishes, most of which are also valuable as food. The istiophorids, together with the swordfish—which is set aside in a separate family—are often referred to as bill-fishes. There are about ten species included in the Istiophoridae; all of them have bills that are rounded in cross section, and have two ridges on each side of the caudal peduncle, just in front of the tail. In contrast, the swordfish has a flattened bill and a single ridge on the caudal peduncle. The sailfish, spearfish, and marlin have ventral fins; this distinguishes them from the swordfish.

Among the istiophorids, the sailfish *(Istiophorus platypterus)* is undoubtedly the most easily recognized because of the extremely long rays of the dorsal fin as well as the dark spots covering the fin. The ventral or pelvic fins are very slender and longer than the pectorals, and they fit into grooves under the body. The sailfish is a worldwide resident of tropical seas. Maximum weight for the Pacific population is around 221 pounds at a length of 11 feet, while those in the Atlantic are much smaller.

218

Swordfish (Xiphias gladius), photographed at 2,000 feet; Atlantic-Pacific marine.

The Pacific shortbill spearfish *(Tetrapturus angustirostris)* looks like a sailfish whose dorsal fin has been trimmed down. Although it reaches a length of 6 feet, it weighs only about 60 pounds. The western Atlantic longbill spearfish *(T. pfleugeri)* is a similar-looking species. The Pacific striped marlin *(T. audax)* is a well-marked species with ten or more vertical stripes along the sides; the body is laterally compressed in the area of the anal fin, which is helpful in differentiating it from other banded marlins.

The Pacific striped marlin is one of the smaller species, having a maximum weight of around 600 pounds, whereas the blue marlin *(Makaira nigricans)*, which occurs both in the Atlantic and in the Pacific, reaches a maximum weight of about 1,400 pounds. In the Atlantic the blue marlin ranges as far north as Long Island. The Atlantic white marlin *(T. albidus)* is another well-known sport species with a maximum size of about 106 pounds and 9 feet.

Swordfish (Family Xiphiidae)

All of the billfishes have respectable nose extensions, but the swordfish *(Xiphias gladius)* carries this development to the extreme, the sword sometimes equaling

Overleaf, top left: Spotted scorpionfish (Scorpaena plumieri); Atlantic marine. Bottom left: Treefish (Sebastes serriceps); Pacific marine. Right: Gopher rockfish (Sebastes carnatus); Pacific marine.

one third of the total length of the fish. It is flattened rather than rounded like the nose extensions of the other billfishes—a feature that is responsible for its being called the broadbill. The sword may be used to impale fishes during feeding, and it can even be driven through the planking of small boats. An attack on the deep-diving submarine Alvin, which is operated by the Woods Hole Oceanographic Institute, at a depth of 1,985 feet, revealed that undersea craft can also be targets, though they are less vulnerable. The world's record weight is held by a swordfish that weighed 1,182 pounds and measured about 15 feet (from Chile, in 1953). The distribution of the one species is worldwide in temperate and tropical seas. Unlike other billfishes, the swordfish lacks pelvic fins.

Discovery of high mercury levels in swordfish has had a disastrous effect on the fishery. Ironically, it is probable that these contamination levels have existed for a number of years without anyone being aware of them.

BUTTERFISHES AND THEIR RELATIVES
(Suborder Stromateoidei)

The fishes of this marine group share an anatomical peculiarity not found among other fishes: they have an expanded and muscular esophagus armed with ridges, papillae, or even teeth. The oval-shaped, laterally compressed harvestfishes lack the pelvic fins as adults and are usually premium food fishes. Along the American Atlantic shores the best-known harvestfish is the 12-inch butterfish, *Peprilus triacanthus;* on the Pacific coast the only northern species is the 10-inch California pompano, *P. simillimus*, really a butterfish and not a pompano at all.

Most of the man-of-war fishes are small and are distinguished from the butterfishes by the fact that they have pelvic fins. The 3-inch man-of-war fish *(Nomeus gronovii)* is worldwide in distribution throughout tropical seas; it is invariably found among the long, stinging tentacles of the giant jellyfishes.

The third type is represented by the smalleye squaretail *(Tetragonurus cuvieri)*, a fish noted for its tough, unremovable scales. It has been aptly described as looking as if it had been carved from wood. It is worldwide in distribution in the depths of tropical and temperate seas.

Scorpionfishes and Rockfishes (Family Scorpaenidae)

This family includes several hundred species, the majority being found in temperate marine waters and a few in tropical seas. Of the approximately 65 species

Leopard searobin (Prionotus scitulus); Atlantic marine.

found on the American Pacific coast, at least 63 occur in the temperate to cold waters of the 850-mile California coast line. Unfortunately, many of these fishes are so difficult to identify accurately that it often requires a specialist to be certain of the species. Most of the scorpaenids spend their time on or near the bottom, often in rocky areas; hence the name "rockfish" or "rockcod." The name "scorpionfish" comes from the venomous nature of the dorsal, anal, and pelvic fin spines, which even without a venom gland can give the careless fisherman a very painful puncture wound. Some species, such as the tropical turkeyfishes, or lionfishes, of the genus *Pterois*, have venom glands in grooves along the sides of each spine. Contact with one of these turkeyfish spines has

Overleaf, left: Female kelp greenling (Hexagrammos decagrammus);
Pacific marine. Right: Skilfish (Erilepis zonifer); Pacific marine.

never resulted in death, although there have been several cases that were almost fatal.

The venom carried by the spines of the California scorpionfish *(Scorpaena guttata)* is almost as virulent as that of the turkeyfish. This species, incidentally, is one of a few in the family that do not bear living young. The California scorpionfish lays a peculiar gelatinous egg balloon that may measure 8 inches in diameter; the individual eggs are embedded in the thin wall of the balloon.

The most deadly of all fish venoms is found in the ugly stonefish *(Synanceia verrucosa)*, a tropical Indo-Pacific species that does not occur in the Americas. The pressure of a swimmer's foot on the half-buried fish can cause the bulbous glands in the fish to eject their neurotoxic venom into his foot. A South African case history reports that one swimmer survived for only two hours after such an incident.

Commercially, most of the scorpaenids are considered good food fishes. In rocky areas they are caught on hook and line, but in open areas and in deep water, trawl nets are used. Trawl nets are also used in catching the redfish, or ocean perch *(Sebastes marinus)*, a species common on both sides of the North Atlantic at depths between 300 and 700 feet.

Searobins *(Family Triglidae)*

The highly colorful searobins have hard, casquelike, bony heads usually equipped with spines. There are two separate dorsal fins; the lower rays of the large fanlike pectoral fins are separate and are used as feelers when the searobin "walks" over the bottom. These fishes are found from shallow to moderate depths in tropical and temperate waters around the world. The largest members of the family range between 2 and 3 feet in length, and the people of some areas consider them excellent food. About 85 species are recognized.

All of the searobins are thought to be able to produce sound; in fact, one of the noisiest fishes on the American Atlantic coast is the 16-inch northern searobin *(Prionotus carolinus)*, which occurs from Nova Scotia to Venezuela.

The armored searobins have their entire bodies covered with heavy plates bearing spines. The snout has two lateral bony projections extending forward as twin fingers. There are barbels attached to the lower jaw, and the pectoral fins have two free rays. Most of the armored searobins are deep-water tropical and temperate marine fishes and are thought to be more sedentary than their cousins, the common or unarmored searobins.

Sablefish and Skilfish (Family Anoplopomatidae)

Two species, both found in deep waters of the North Pacific, are the only members of this family: the 3-foot sablefish *(Anoplopoma fimbria)* and the rare 6-foot skilfish *(Erilepis zonifer)*. The sablefish is fished commercially; its flesh is excellent when smoked. The preferred habitat of the sablefish is at the edge of the continental shelf and there are records of tagged fish having traveled as much as 1,200 miles. The distribution for both species ranges from Alaska to California.

Greenlings (Family Hexagrammidae)

The greenlings form a small family of North Pacific cold-water marine species. They are often brightly colored and have smooth heads, usually with one cirrus, or whisker, over each eye. Some of the larger species are excellent food fishes. The kelp greenling *(Hexagrammos decagrammus)* is noted for the fact that the male and female have conspicuously different color patterns. This species reachs a length of 21 inches and ranges from Alaska to southern California. The lingcod *(Ophiodon elongatus)* has about the same geographic range, and partly because of its large size (up to 5 feet and 100 pounds), it is fished commercially. Divers often encounter the 6- to 10-inch painted greenling *(Oxylebius pictus)*, sometimes called the convict fish; this species has an immunity to the stinging cells of the giant *Telia* anemones which are often abundant in the *Oxylebius* habitat. A very strange behavior pattern has been recorded for the 10-inch shortspine and longspine combfishes of the genus *Zaniolepis*. When first dumped on the deck from a trawling net, combfishes react by attempting to take their own tails into their mouths, and for a short period of time the body has a U-shaped configuration. No explanation is known for this activity.

Sculpins (Family Cottidae)

The cottids, a group of some 300 species, are mostly bottom-dwelling fishes, often scaleless or partially scaled. Many are marine fishes found in cold northern waters. Some sculpins survive well in brackish water, and a number live only in fresh water. The sculpins have two dorsal fins, either separate or with a notch between the spiny-rayed and soft-rayed portions. The pectoral fins are fan-shaped and quite large, and the pelvics, if present, usually have a spine and

Overleaf, left: Painted greenling (Oxylebius pictus). Right, top to bottom:
Lingcod (Ophiodon elongatus). Grunt sculpin (Rhamphocottus richardsoni).
Cabezon (Scorpaenichthys marmoratus); All, Pacific marine. Longhorn
sculpin (Myoxocephalus octodecimspinosus); Atlantic marine.

from two to five soft rays. A characteristic American Pacific type is the 20-inch red Irish lord *(Hemilepidotus hemilepidotus)*.

One of the largest sculpins is the crab-eating cabezon *(Scorpaenichthys marmoratus)*, a species that reaches a length of 30 inches and a weight of 25 pounds. Its normal range is from British Columbia to Baja California. Despite the peculiar color of its flesh—often green—the cabezon is good to eat, but its roe is poisonous. Undoubtedly the most common shallow-water, western American marine cottid is the Pacific staghorn sculpin *(Leptocottus armatus)*, a species having hooks on the opercle; it is abundant in bays all the way from Alaska to Baja California. Most of those encountered are smaller than 6 inches, but occasionally an individual may reach 12 inches.

The American Atlantic sea raven *(Hemitripterus americanus)* has the surprising ability to swallow air and blow up like a balloon when removed from the water. When thrown back into the water, it floats helplessly until it is able to release the air; it is not known why the air is not released immediately. The sailfin sculpin *(Nautichthys oculofasciatus)*, from the shores of Pacific northwest America, is a cottid with a startling appearance. The first five rays of the dorsal fin are greatly elongated, and the fish often erects them over its head like a tremendous sail.

One of the largest of the many American fresh-water species is the 12-inch prickly sculpin *(Cottus asper)*, which ranges from southern California to Alaska.

The grunt sculpin *(Rhamphocottus richardsoni)* is probably the world's most comical fish. As it moves across the bottom, each movement is a series of short jumps aided by the finger-like tips of the pectoral fins. When in a hurry, the grunt swims up from the bottom with all the grace of a captive blimp that has just broken its moorings. The independent motion of the eyes, each moving without reference to the other, adds to its strange appearance. The name "grunt" comes from the noise produced when *Rhamphocottus* is removed from the water. This small 3-inch fish is found along the American Pacific coast from Alaska to California. In captivity the grunt sculpin does well, living for several years, provided the temperature of the water is kept below 55° and sufficient food is available in the form of small crustaceans.

Poachers and Alligatorfishes (Family Agonidae)

The cold-water marine poachers and their relatives look much like some of the South American fresh-water armored catfishes of the family Loricariidae, but the two families are not related. The poachers usually have elongated bodies covered with bony plates; the edges of the individual plates are often saw-toothed. The pelvic fins are generally located just behind the pectorals in a thoracic position; these pelvic fins as well as the second dorsal and anal fins are sometimes longer in the males than in the females. The agonids live on the bottom; a few live in tide pools, but the majority are found in deeper water, down as much as 2,000 feet. These are Northern Hemisphere fishes, most of the species occurring in the North Pacific, with at least sixteen species in California.

Lumpfishes and Snailfishes (Family Cyclopteridae)

Members of this family usually have modified pelvic fins that form a sucking disk located under the body and directly behind the head. Lumpfishes have large tubercles on the outside of the body, whereas snailfishes have small prickles on the body or have a smooth skin. The lumpfish body is globose rather than elongate, and the dorsal fin is usually divided by a notch into two sections. Lumpsuckers are carnivorous, cold-water marine fishes found only in the Northern Hemisphere. On the American Pacific coast they occur as far south as the Puget Sound area, the southernmost species being the 5-inch spiny lump-sucker *(Eumicrotremus orbis)*.

The elongate snailfishes usually have a flabby, jelly-like skin. The very long dorsal fin starts a short distance behind the head and has a few spiny rays at its anterior end. Like the lumpfishes, these are carnivorous, cold-water marine forms seldom found in water warmer than 60°. Some 115 species of these bottom fishes are recognized. There are about six species in the tropical Pacific, five in the Antarctic, fourteen in the North Atlantic, and the remainder—about three fourths of those known—in the North Pacific. They are found at depths ranging from the very shallow water of tide pools to two miles down. Most species are full grown at a length of less than 7 inches, but there are a few that reach 12 inches.

FLYING GURNARDS (Order Dactylopteriformes)

Although the flying gurnards bear a resemblance to the searobins, they are placed in a separate order because of certain primitive characteristics in the arrangement of the head bones. There are only a few species of these tropical marine fishes. Like the searobins, they are bottom forms. Identification of the flying gurnards is relatively easy because of their outstanding characteristics: tremendously enlarged pectoral fins with the inner rays free, a large bony head, and a single isolated dorsal spine attached to the nape of the neck. Much remains to be learned about their so-called flying ability. According to some, they are able to propel themselves out of the water and make an ineffectual attempt at flight. However, photographic documentation of this activity, such as that available on the flight of the true flyingfishes, remains to be gathered. *Dactylopterus volitans*, which reaches a length of 18 inches, has a wide distribution on both sides of the Atlantic.

FLATFISHES (Order Pleuronectiformes)

When the young flatfish is hatched from its floating egg, it acts like any other larval fish and swims with its body in a normal position. Within a few days, however, something strange begins to happen: one eye starts moving to the opposite side of the head, and soon the larval flatfish has two eyes on the same side. The dorsal fin then begins to grow forward on the head. In many species the mouth becomes twisted and the pectoral fins become unequal in size. About this time the young flatfish sinks to the ocean bottom, where it will spend most of the remainder of its life lying on its blind side, with its eyed side up. The blind side of the body does not develop pigment and so is usually whitish in color. In some flatfishes it is always the right eye that migrates to the opposite side; in others it is always the left eye; and in still others, either eye may make this migration. If both eyes are on the right side of the head, the flatfish is known as a right-eyed or dextral fish; if both eyes are on the left side, it is called a left-eyed or sinistral fish. To further complicate the matter, in certain flatfishes, such as the Pacific starry flounder *(Platichthys stellatus)*, this characteristic may vary with locality.

Included among the flatfishes are many of the world's most valuable food species, such as halibut, flounder, plaice, turbot, and sole. These, however, are only a few of the approximately 600 species that have been described in this important group. These fishes are chiefly marine and are carnivorous in their food habits. They range in size from very small species only a few inches in length to giants of 10 feet weighing 700 pounds. The majority occur in all but the coldest seas, in shallow water or in moderate depths; a few are found at great depths.

Top: Kelp poacher (undescribed); Pacific marine.
Bottom: Pithead poacher (Bothragonus swani); Pacific marine.

found in the brackish water of estuaries and in some areas actually enters fresh water. In Japan, for example, it is found in certain lakes and rivers.

The name "turbot" is applied to deep-bodied members of various genera of flatfishes. The 12-inch curlfin turbot *(Pleuronichthys decurrens)* is one of the most desirable of the American Pacific species. A related species in the same area, *P. coenosus*, is known as the CO sole because of a CO-shaped mark on the side of the caudal peduncle.

Soles (Family Soleidae)

The term "filet of sole" was originally applied to the common European sole *(Solea solea)* but now is loosely used for any kind of fileted flatfish. In the true soles both eyes are on the right side of the head, and the preopercular margin of the gill cover is never free but is hidden by the skin and scales of the head. These fishes are ribless, and some have interesting patterns, such as the naked sole *(Gymnachirus melas)*, a striped species of the American Atlantic coast.

Also included in this group is the 6-inch hogchoker *(Trinectes maculatus)*, a marine species that is often found in fresh water and occurs from North Carolina to Panama. It has transverse lines across the body and, strangely enough, has a spotted pattern on the blind side.

Tonguefishes (Family Cynoglossidae)

Eyes on the left side of the head, a pointed tail, and the absence of ribs are characteristics that readily identify the tonguefishes. In some respects, these fishes resemble the true soles of the previous family, but true soles have the eyes on the right side of the head and have a small tail fin that is not pointed. The tonguefishes are a small, teardrop-shaped, inconspicuous species, usually less than 12 inches in length. A few of the larger species in Japan and other areas are used for food, but most members of the family are too small to be of value as market fishes.

TRIGGERFISHES, PUFFERS, OCEAN SUNFISHES, AND THEIR RELATIVES (Order Tetraodontiformes)

Although the tetraodontiforms probably descended from a surgeonfish-like ancestor, there is little in the external appearance of these peculiar fishes to

Overleaf, left, top to bottom: Whitespotted filefish (Cantherhines macrocerus); Atlantic marine. Fringed filefish (Monacanthus ciliatus); Atlantic marine. Redtail trigger (Xanthichthys mento); Pacific marine. Right: Queen triggerfish (Balistes vetula); Atlantic marine.

Lefteye Flounders (Family Bothidae)

Most of the lefteye or bothid flounders are of moderate size and are found from shallow to deep ocean water. Some, such as the American Atlantic peacock flounder *(Bothus lunatus)*, have very attractive patterns. The application of the common name "sole" to some members of this family, such as the American Pacific fantail sole *(Xystreurys liolepis)*, is a constant source of confusion, because the only true soles are those belonging to another family, the Soleidae. The confusion is further compounded by the use of this name for some of the righteye flounders of the family Pleuronectidae.

The small sanddabs of the genus *Citharichthys* are well-known American Pacific lefteye flounders and are usually listed on the menus of seafood restaurants. The Pacific sanddab *(C. sordidus)* is the most common species. The ocellated flounders are a striking group of three American Atlantic species assigned to the genus *Ancylopsetta*. Two of the species have three large ocelli on the eyed side of the body, and the third one, the 10-inch *A. quadrocellata*, has four. The latter is a shallow-water form ranging from North Carolina through the Gulf of Mexico.

Righteye Flounders (Family Pleuronectidae)

The International Fisheries Commission, through careful study of the giant Pacific halibut (*Hippoglossus stenolepsis*), was able to regulate this fishery, which had been depleted, so that both the total catch and the yield to the individual fisherman were greatly increased. The story of the Pacific halibut is often cited to show that careful biological study can help the yield of depleted fisheries.

Pacific halibut females may reach a weight of 470 pounds at an age of 35 years; they grow much faster than the relatively puny males, which after 25 years weigh only 40 pounds. With growth, they move into deep water. Pacific halibut are found all the way from northern California to northwestern Alaska, but the most productive grounds are from Washington northward. Even larger than the Pacific halibut is its cousin, the Atlantic halibut *(H. hippoglossus)*, reported to reach a weight of 700 pounds and an age of 40 years. It occurs on both sides of the North Atlantic southward to the Bay of Biscay on the European side and to New York on the American side.

Most of the pleuronectids are marine species living on coastal shelves. One exception is the Pacific starry flounder *(Platichthys stellatus)*, which is often

indicate this relationship. All of them have small openings from the gill cavities and small mouths with strong teeth. A few have scales; others have bony plates, spines or a leathery skin. These carnivorous fishes live in all tropical marine waters, and a few stray into cooler seas. A large number of these fishes have poisonous organs and flesh, but in spite of this they are eaten regularly in some parts of the world, occasionally with fatal results. The five best-known families are discussed below.

Triggerfishes and Filefishes (Family Balistidae)

Triggerfishes receive their name from the locking mechanism of the first and second dorsal fin spines. When the long first dorsal spine is erected, the second, which is very small, moves forward and locks the first into an upright position. A frightened triggerfish reacts by diving into a coral head and erecting the spine, thus insuring its safety from predators or ichthyological collectors, who cannot remove the fish without breaking down the coral. The small second trigger spine must be released before the large first spine can be depressed. Triggers have an outer series of eight teeth in each jaw as well as an inner series of six platelike teeth in the upper jaw. The pelvic fins are lacking, but a pelvic spine is usually present. Triggers are shallow-water, tropical marine species, usually solitary and slow-moving in their habits. Some are noise makers; when removed from the water, they make a grunting sound that is produced by the air bladder.

Typical of the family is the beautiful 17-inch queen trigger *(Balistes vetula)*, which occurs on both sides of the tropical and temperate Atlantic.

The tropical marine filefishes resemble the triggers but have much narrower bodies. The first dorsal spine is placed farther forward, usually over the eyes, whereas in the trigger it is to the rear of the eyes. The pelvic fins are lacking. Between the chin and the anal fin there is a well-developed, usually distensible, pelvic flap that looks like a dewlap. Many of the filefishes are full grown at a length of 5 to 10 inches, but the longtail filefish *(Alutera scripta)*, the largest species in the family, may reach a length of 40 inches. About 120 species of triggers and files are recognized.

Puffers (Family Tetraodontidae)

When a puffer is pulled from the water, it immediately reacts—like the American

Atlantic sea raven—by swallowing air so that it quickly blows up like a balloon. An expanded puffer thrown back into the water floats upside down for several minutes or sometimes much longer before it is able to expel the air and return to its normal swimming condition. Puffers can also swallow water in the same way they swallow air. The puffers form a large group of about 100 species of carnivorous fishes found throughout all warm and most temperate seas. Their maximum size is 36 inches, but the majority of the species are fully grown at less than 18 inches. The 10-inch checkered puffer *(Sphoeroides testudineus)* is a representative species ranging from New England to southeastern Brazil.

The sharpnose puffers are seldom larger than 5 inches; they have a long, narrow nose, somewhat sharp and with inconspicuous nostrils. The body is slightly compressed, and the external gill openings are very small—about half the length of the pectoral fin base. All of these features distinguish the small sharpnose puffers from the common puffers. A dozen species are found in tropical seas around the world; because of their small size, they are popular with tropical fish hobbyists.

Porcupinefishes and Burrfishes (Family Diodontidae)

A newcomer making his first trip through Chinatown in San Francisco usually stops to admire one of the large, conspicuous balloon lamps covered with spines. Close examination shows that it is the dried outside skin of a porcupinefish with a light bulb placed inside. The porcupinefish, or balloonfish, is actually a puffer with spines on the outside of the body. The species with large spines hold them in against the body while swimming, and it is only when they begin to swallow air or water that the spines are fully evident. The small burrfishes of the genus *Chilomycterus*, sometimes called spiny boxfishes, have short spines that are immovable and always extended. About fifteen kinds of porcupinefishes and burrfishes are known from the tropical marine waters of the world.

Trunkfishes (Family Ostraciidae)

A trunkfish, sometimes called a cowfish or a boxfish, can be aptly described as a solid bony box with holes for the mouth, eyes, fins, and vent. Generic identification of the trunkfishes is based on the contours of the outside skeleton —whether it has three, four, or five angles and whether there are spines over the eyes. Identification is complicated by the fact that the males and females

Striped burrfish (Chilomycterus schoepfi); Atlantic marine.
Overleaf, top left: Checkered pufferfish (Sphoeroides testudineus); Atlantic
marine. Bottom left: Spotted trunkfish (Lactophrys bicaudalis) with remora;
Atlantic marine. Right: Balloonfish (Diodon holocanthus); Atlantic marine.

of a single species may have different color patterns. Most species are small, 24 inches being the maximum length attained. Some thirty species are recognized. Several of the American Atlantic species have wide ranges from New England to Brazil.

In the Hawaiian Islands, the late Vernon Brock showed that these fishes, when handled, sometimes discharge a toxin that kills other fishes kept in the same container. The water retains the unknown toxin even after all fishes are removed.

Ocean Sunfishes (Family Molidae)

The ocean sunfish looks like a giant puffer that has had the posterior half of its vertically-compressed body chopped off just behind the high dorsal and anal fins. There is a tail fin at the end of the truncated body, but one must look carefully to find it. The pelvic bones and pelvic fins are lacking. The larval ocean sunfish has a number of spiny projections and does not even slightly resemble the adult. It swims like a normal fish—that is, vertically—and the fast-moving juveniles also swim this way. As they grow older, the sunfishes spend much of the time on their sides, lazily flapping the high dorsal or anal fin out of the water. A full-grown common ocean sunfish *(Mola mola)* may measure 11 feet in length and weigh as much as 2,000 pounds. Two other species are included in the family.

EXTERNAL VIEW OF SHARK

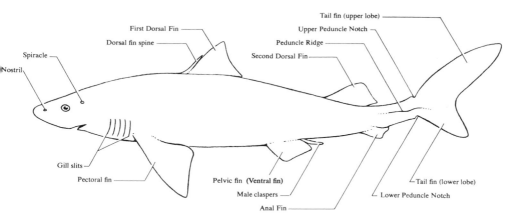

INTERNAL ANATOMY OF A SOFT-RAYED FISH (TROUT OR SALMON)

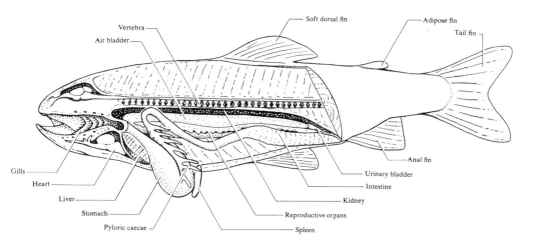

EXTERNAL VIEW OF A SPINY-RAYED FISH (MACKEREL OR TUNA TYPE)

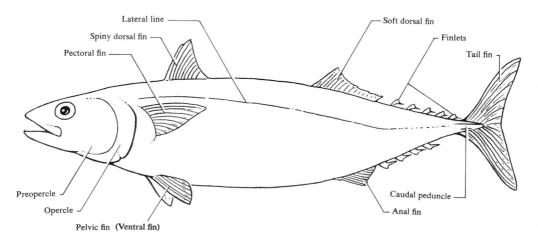

Glossary

Abdomen. Belly.

Adipose fin. A small, fleshy fin, without rays, located behind the dorsal fin on the back of some fishes.

Air bladder. A gas-filled sac located in the body cavity below the vertebrae; also called a swim bladder.

Anal fin. The fin on the median ventral line behind the anus.

Anterior. In front of, or toward, the head.

Anus. The vent.

Barbel. A slender, tactile, whisker-like projection extending from the head of some fishes.

Branchial. Pertaining to the gills.

Buckler. A bony shield.

Canine tooth. Elongated conical tooth.

Caudal. Pertaining to the tail.

Caudal fin. The tail fin.

Caudal peduncle. The slender portion of the fish's body just in front of the tail fin.

Ciguatera. A toxemia caused by eating the flesh of certain fishes.

Cirri. Fringelike tendrils, whiskers, or tufts of skin.

Clasper. One of a pair of elongated reproductive organs on the pelvic fins of male sharks, skates, rays, and ratfishes.

Cleaner. A fish or invertebrate that attaches itself to and removes parasites from other larger fish.

Dorsal fin. A fin on the back.

Finlet. A small, usually separate fin ray located in a series behind the main dorsal or anal fin.

Fry. The young of fishes.

Gill arch. The bony support to which gills are attached.

Gill cover. A lid or flap covering the gill; also called an opercle or operculum.

Gill filament. A threadlike structure attached to the outside of a gill arch.

Gill opening. The opening leading from the gills; also called the gill cleft.

Gill raker. A bony projection attached to the inside of gill arches; used to strain food from the water.

Gill. A filamentous respiratory organ of aquatic animals.

Gonad. A sexual organ: an ovary, a testis, or a hermaphrodite gland.

Gonopodium. The modified anal fin in its function as a copulatory organ in certain fishes.

Gular plate. A hard plate covering the under part of the chin between the lower jaws; present in some fishes.

Incisor. A front tooth flattened to the form of a cutting edge.

Jugular. Pertaining to the neck or throat.

Lateral. Pertaining to the side.

Lateral line. The longitudinal line on each side of a fish's body, composed of pores opening into sensory organs.

Mandible. The lower jaw.

Maxillary. The second and usually the larger of the two bones forming the upper jaw.

Milt. The sperm of fishes.

Molar. A grinding tooth.

Nictitating membrane. A membrane that assists in keeping the eye clean in reptiles, birds, mammals, and in some sharks and bony fishes; sometimes called a third eyelid.

246

Opercle. A gill cover; also called an operculum.

Opercular flap. A fleshy extension of the rear edge of the opercle.

Osseous. Bony.

Otolith. One of two or three small, somewhat spherical bones found in the inner ear of fishes

Ovary. A female reproductive gland.

Oviparous. Egg-laying, with the eggs hatching outside of body.

Ovoviviparous. Producing eggs with definite shells that hatch within the body of the female, so that the young are born alive.

Pectoral fin. One of a pair of fins attached to the shoulder girdle.

Pelvic or **ventral fin.** One of a pair of fins below the pectoral fins.

Pelvic girdle. The bones supporting the pelvic fins.

Pharyngeal tooth. A grinding tooth located in the pharynx, on the last gill arch.

Pharynx. The section of the alimentary canal joining the mouth cavity to the esophagus.

Photophore. A luminous or light-producing organ or spot.

Premaxillary. One of a pair of bones forming the front of the upper jaw in fishes.

Preopercle. The anterior cheekbone.

Protractile. Capable of being thrust forward.

Pseudobranchia. A small gill-like structure on the inner side of the gill cover.

Roe. The eggs of fishes.

Scute. An external horny or bony plate or scale.

Soft ray. A flexible, jointed ray.

Spiny ray. A very hard, non-jointed spine, usually pointed.

Spiracle. A small respiratory opening behind the eye in sharks, skates, and rays.

Spiral valve. A corkscrew-like partition in the digestive tract.

Swim bladder. An air bladder.

Testis. A male reproductive gland.

Thoracic. Pertaining to the thorax, or chest.

Ventral fin. A pelvic fin.

Vent. The external opening of the intestine; also called the anus.

Vertical fin. An unpaired fin along the median line of the body, such as the dorsal, anal, or caudal fin.

Vestigial. Small and imperfectly developed; rudimentary.

Viviparous. Bringing forth young alive.

Vomer. The median bone in the front upper part of the mouth.

Weberian ossicles. A chain of four small bones connecting the air bladder with the ear in the order Ostariophysi.

Index

Asterisks indicate pages containing illustrations.

248

251

253

254

CREDITS

The Animal Life of North America series (six volumes) is prepared and produced
by Chanticleer Press:
Publisher: Paul Steiner
Editor: Milton Rugoff. *Associates:* Susan Weiley, Joanne Shapiro, Jean Walker
Art Director: Ulrich Ruchti, assisted by Roberta Savage
Production: Gudrun Buettner, assisted by Helga Lose
Printed by Amilcare Pizzi, S.p.A., Milan, Italy